THE GR FACTOR

Unleashing the Undeniable Power of the
Golden Rule

Table of Contents

THE GR FACTOR

Unleashing the Undeniable Power of the
Golden Rule

Jack R. Nerad

E.M. Landsea Publishers LLC is a proponent of free speech and the open exchange of ideas. It also is a strong supporter of copyright as a key component of free speech.

Vignettes within this book are used to illustrate principles and are not designed to represent individuals.

E.M. Landsea Publishers LLC
Chicago | New York | Los Angeles

ISBN: 9781732687639

To my brother Eric who has supported the writing of this book
every step of the way

Chapter One

Establishing the Premise

Achieving success in business is difficult. I'm not here to tell you it isn't. And I'm not here to tell you it can be accomplished with little effort. Business is hard. Customers are demanding; competition is never-ending, and change is forever with us. It is a constant struggle. But while it may be very challenging for each individual engaged in business, for society as a whole the struggle is good because the rigors of doing business weed out poor products and the organizations that attempt to exploit customers rather than to serve them. But what is good for society makes it difficult for those engaged in commerce.

Take it from someone who has done it, starting your own business is hard. Sustaining it is even harder. And I've had successes and failures in my own endeavors to prove that. At the same time, working in someone else's business is hard, because winning and keeping your superiors' respect is an ongoing challenge. Typically they will never like you as much as they like themselves. And often maintaining your respect for them in the face of their actions that you don't agree with is even harder.

Establishing and maintaining good relationships with co-workers is hard. Each of us is the product of our unique background and upbringing. We have different value systems. We are motivated by different things. Our worldviews can be radically askew and yet in a business context people need to work together. The rigors of business make it extremely difficult to succeed if employees of an organization can't find common ground.

Some people are good and motivated by the best intentions. Others are evil and actively pursue evil ends. Many are somewhere in the middle, trying to do what is best for all but at the same time operating in a self-serving manner much of the time. When it comes to a decision between the best interests of the enterprise and the best interests of themselves, they will take themselves every day of the week. In some ways they can't be blamed because in most large organizations, when it comes to a decision between the best interests of the enterprise and the best interests of the individual employees, the managers of the organization will take the enterprise's interests — or more to the point the perceived best interests of the top managers — every day of the week. A lot is said about company loyalty, but when push comes to shove company loyalty usually means the company managers are loyal to themselves.

So with all these obstacles to success in business, how does a business owner, a CEO, a middle manager and an individual employee overcome them to prosper? How can owners, managers and employees find common ground that will enable success?

That is what I intend to reveal — at length and in practical steps — in this book. The GR Factor is that common ground. It is that transformative, "oh-yeah" doctrine that will make all else fade into the background.

If you apply the GR Factor to your business and to your life, it will be transformative. You and your business will emerge from the dark shadows of doubt and distrust and enter the light of true cooperation. You will progress from living a life of negatives to living a life of positives.

The goal is finding the good and enabling it to overcome the bad. Oh, the negatives will still be out there waiting to trip you up. The bad will continue to exist among us. But the GR Factor will give you the tools to triumph over the negatives, to float above the detractors and to achieve genuine success. In fact it will give you the vision to see what real success looks like.

For many of us, each workday is a struggle. We find ourselves in situations we don't like, working with people we don't care for, and we are unmotivated to do our best work and be our best selves. Deep down we picture ourselves as victims. But if we are victims we are victims of circumstances every human being faces every day. It is difficult to make the case that is genuine victimhood.

With the GR Factor in your life, you will see things differently, because you will have a deeper understanding of your most precious humanity. You will begin approaching each new day as an opportunity, not as a problem. Each day will be a new chance to realize your best potential, not just another twenty-four hours to survive.

Challenges will continue to come your way. New competitors will spring up. New hires in your organization will upset the previous norm and send shockwaves rippling through the enterprise. Natural disasters will occur without warning. You might lose your job or, more to the point, your job might lose you.

But if you follow the simple tenets of the GR Factor as I outline them, you will have an answer to all these challenges and more. You will have a toolkit filled with the keys to real success. And you will be able to face down and overcome adversity with confidence inspired by the self-respect that you have justly earned.

In business and in life, we have two stark choices before us: we can conduct ourselves as animals whose overriding instinct is self-gratification or we can conduct ourselves on the highest plane of humanity with respect, admiration and love for one another.

If you choose the latter way by applying the GR Factor in your life it will enable you to understand what others want by examining what you want. In the following pages, we'll tell you how to do that in all of your life situations. It has the true power to bring you business success and transform your life.

"The wind blows where it wishes, and you hear the sound of it, but cannot tell where it comes from and where it goes. So is everyone who is born of the Spirit." (John 3:6-8)

Chapter Two

What this is all about

Most books that offer advice take a leisurely time getting to the key point. Typically there is a long ramp-up to the punchline. You learn a little – or a lot – about the author's youth, hear something about his or her business experience and then get a slow waltz to the BIG MESSAGE. As has been said so frequently about so many things, there's nothing wrong with that, but I've decided to spare you all the preliminaries. Instead, here it is up front. Based on my forty years of success in various aspects of business here is the essential piece of advice I have to deliver.

This is what I call The GR Factor:

Treat other people the way you want to be treated.

In fact, this is so vitally important for you to know and remember, let me repeat it for emphasis.

Treat other people the way you want to be treated.

If you apply this principle every minute of every day of your life – or as close to that as a human can muster the will to do it – I guarantee you will be successful in business. You will find success running your own business and you will find success as an executive and manager in a business owned by others. Most importantly, you will find fulfillment and joy in your personal life. Every day.

How do I know this? I know this because it has worked for me, and because I have seen it work for others as well. It is a philosophy, a way of life, that breeds success.

If you want to close the book right now, you can – as long as you take to heart the message of treating others as you'd like to be treated and, critically, don't simply look at that precept as a tool or a technique to be turned on and off like a light switch, but instead make it a vital part of your essential being. In others words, don't just do it – LIVE IT.

If you can do that, feel free to close the book now. You will have received untold value from the price you paid for this advice, and it might be all you need. You can save yourself the time it will take to read the rest of what I've written for you.

But if you are intrigued by this advice or are skeptical that guidance so simple can have a life-changing effect, then I invite you to read on. What I expect to demonstrate to you in the following pages is how this works and why this works IN A BUSINESS CONTEXT. And though you have probably read or heard this advice or something quite like it before, I doubt very much that you have heard it spelled out as a way of furthering your personal success in commerce and industry. And that is what I will concentrate on delivering in the upcoming chapters.

Certainly I am not the first to offer this advice. Those of you who are either religious and/or have studied religion have no doubt come across this counsel many times. In the widely used King James version of the *Bible*, Jesus Christ said, "And as ye would that men should do to you, do ye also to them likewise." In the New American Standard version of the *Bible*, which uses our common vernacular, the same verse says, "Treat others the same way you want them to treat you."

By way of full disclosure, I am a practicing Christian, and I have tried to abide by this rule for the past fifty years. But a study of other religions and belief systems reveals that this concept is not unique to the New Testament, Christianity or even the Judeo-Christian tradition. Old Testament Leviticus 19:34 is highly studied and often quoted by Jewish scholars. The verse says, "The stranger who resides with you shall be to you as one of your citizens; you shall love him as yourself, for you were strangers in the land of Egypt: I the LORD am your God." Slightly earlier in Leviticus (19:18) is the message "You shall not take vengeance or bear a grudge against your kinsfolk. Love your neighbor as yourself: I am the LORD."

Right now you might be saying to yourself, "I thought I was going to get advice that would help me with my business. I'm not here for *Bible* study." That's fair. But I'm not quoting the *Bible* for the sake of promulgating religious beliefs. I'm quoting the *Bible* to demonstrate how pervasive this simple idea is as a style of living. Further, I'm proposing to you that adopting this style of living in your business activities is the key to success.

I can quote you similar verses ascribed to Buddha, to Muhammad, to Confucius, to the Greeks Thales and Sextus the Pythagorean. (Yes, even Sextus the Pythagorean.) You will find similar admonitions in the *Pahlavi Texts* of Zoroastrianism, the *Tirukkural* of the Tamil Tradition, the *Torah*, the *Talmud*, the *New Testament* of the *Bible* and the *Quran*. There are subtle differences in the messages and perhaps less subtle differences in how the messages are understood and, importantly, practiced, but there is no doubt that many of the great philosophers, religious leaders, prophets and even the Savior Himself found the ideal of treating others as one would like to be treated as important – and often central – to the daily observation of a religious life.

You might say, "I am not religious; I don't care who in the deep, dark past uttered this mumbo-jumbo. I live in the present."

To you I would make two observations. First, religious observance dates back to the beginning of recorded human history, and it continues to be an important part of the daily life of millions of your contemporaries. It is not an anachronism. Second, for those who do not believe in a God or in religion at all, it is important to grasp that two of the world's most prevalent secular philosophies – Existentialism and Humanism – pay some homage to the simple entreaty to behave in a manner that promotes the greater good. The Humanist philosophy is, arguably, more explicit in suggesting that doing good for others is to be encouraged, while the Existentialists (those darn Existentialists) center their thinking around the fact (hope?) that if individuals make their choices wisely they will always trend toward what is best for the largest number.

Again, all this is cited not in the attempt to promote a single religion or philosophy, but instead to demonstrate that the guiding premise of this book, which is designed to improve your business fortunes, is a premise that has deep roots in antiquity and, at the same time, is widely expressed and believed today. Again, if at this point you say, "I got it," and you close the book, you will reap the many benefits of adhering to this style of living IF YOU ACT ON IT DAILY.

And this is where I believe I can provide help. Many of you might be thinking, yes, I've heard that before, sounds reasonable, but in my daily life, and especially in my business life, I can't act that way. I'd be nothing but a pushover; in minutes I'd be crushed by more aggressive, "me-first" competitors. In today's environment it is perhaps logical to feel that way. The prevailing attitude seems to be "do whatever it takes.

But that is where I believe today's attitudes and the behavior they prompt are very wrong, and the purpose of the remainder of this book is to prove that to you…and to demonstrate to you how treating others as you want to be treated is indeed the best way for business success.

"And the second, like it, is this: 'You shall love your neighbor as yourself.' There is no other commandment greater than these." (Mark 12:31)

"The work of righteousness will be peace, And the effect of righteousness, quietness and assurance forever." (Isaiah 32:17)

Chapter Three

How do we want to be treated?

To suggest to you that you "treat others as you want to be treated" begs the obvious question, "how do you want to be treated?" And the answer is not as simple as you might believe at first blush. Consider the question seriously for a moment. At first you might believe that you want to lead a stressless life of comfort and ease, a life in which no burdens are placed upon you. That way you would have all the time in the world to do what you want to do. But if you consider this for a moment, do you want to lead a life in which you are pampered, coddled, medicated and fed fresh grapes peeled by nubile virgins? No, really, do you? Yes, it might appear appealing at first glance, but how long do you think you could remain happy in a challenge-free environment? Looking at the issue through an adult lens, would you be fulfilled with a life of pure hedonism? Or is the way you'd genuinely like to live your life a manner that offers you the self-respect and self-fulfillment of contributing to a just, caring society?

While a life of narcissistic pleasure-seeking might seem desirable at first glance, psychologists will tell you that individuals who live in circumstances approximating it typically develop a lot of problems. Rather than finding fulfillment in hedonism, individuals come to feel that their lives are purposeless and empty. Studies have shown people typically discover more personal happiness from behaviors that enhance their sense of self worth, and a generally acknowledged way to improve your sense of worth is by helping others.

This is not to imply, however, that every waking minute should be devoted to the service of others with no regard for ourselves and our own well-being. That style of living won't lead to overall happiness either, because while basing all our decisions around our personal desires is a trap that will ultimately lead to alienation from others, doing the exact opposite — basing all our efforts on pleasing others — may lead to complete loss of self. In other words, some "me-time" that doesn't negatively impact others is good. One just needs to avoid the "all-me-all-the-time" mindset and behavior pattern that so many have adopted these days.

So how do we want to be treated? If you ask this question, many are likely to respond that they want to be treated fairly. The difficult part of that desire is to determine what is "fair." To many it equates with being treated the same way as everyone else — no special treatment good or bad. But to others it means getting all the advantages or perceived advantages they view others are receiving. Peeling back the onion, what they seek isn't "fairness," it is unfair advantages that are in their favor rather than against them.

Since I was a small child I heard from my mother and father that "life is not fair," and I'm sure I'm not alone in that. Musings on the unfairness of life abound through religious texts, the works of the great philosophers and on to the essays and screeds populating the corners of the Internet.

Since the sense of what is fair and what is not on a human scale is subjective, it seems that one's place on the fairness-unfairness scale is equally subjective and, all other things being equal (and we know they are not) individuals will look at particular circumstances in their life as being unfair to them largely because they seem more favorable to others.

Take this example from my life. When I was a pre-teen I wanted a gasoline-powered go kart. A couple of other kids in the neighborhood had them, and I thought it would be cool to have one. I started saving up my money to buy one, perhaps with the hope that my parents would kick in a little money, too. But somewhere into this process my parents told me succinctly, "No go kart." I'm not sure why, but I suspect now that I was told no for financial reasons; we as a family simply didn't have the money to afford a moderately expensive toy like a go kart at that time.

So other kids in the neighborhood had go karts, and I didn't — and couldn't — have a go kart. I guess you could say that is unfair. I might even have told my parents I thought it was unfair to which, if parental responses follow true-to-form, they would've replied, "We know, and as we have told you before, life is not fair.'"

But looking back at it through the long lens of time, I now do not consider that my pre-teen inability to obtain a go kart was even mildly unfair to me. Yes, others my age had go karts and I didn't. Seems unfair, I guess. But that is only if you consider go kart/lack of go kart to be the central issue on what one considers fairness. In those terms I was the aggrieved party. Others had go karts; I didn't. "That's unfair to me," I might have claimed.

But when I look back at all the circumstances of my youth versus others, despite my heinous lack of a go kart, I have to believe that life was no more unfair to me than it was to anyone else in my circumstances and by many measures I had advantages that could be considered unfair to others. For instance, I had two loving parents with high moral principles who communicated both love and ethical boundaries to me and to my brother. In retrospect, that alone is far more valuable than having a go kart.

So, again, peering at this through the perspective gained from decades on this planet, I have come to believe two things: First, from our Earthly perch as human beings it is impossible to determine what is fair and what isn't. Second, most people who say they are seeking fairness are actually in need of mercy.

An important thing to understand about mercy is that mercy is typically not earned; it is received as a gift. The recipient of mercy may well not deserve it based on their words and their behavior, but granting mercy has immense benefits for both the donor and the recipient. In the vernacular you might describe mercy as "giving someone the benefit of the doubt." And I think that's what all of us want. We want to be given the benefit of the doubt.

Many of us like to present a strong, positive, self-assured image to the world. We find it appealing to revel in our independence, make our own choices and live our own lives. The "Man of Action" has now been joined by the "Independent Woman" as the templates of preferred, admired lifestyles. While community gains lip-service from many, the "primacy of me" is the lifestyle that seems to dominate popular culture.

"I had to be true to myself."

"When I looked at all the options, I did what I had to do."

"You only live once."

Certainly, having the power to make your own decisions is valuable, but if that power enables you to constantly choose yourself over others, it will soon become destructive not only to those around you, but especially to you. Selfish people sabotage their opportunities for positive long-term relationships. The few long-term relationships they do develop are very likely to be destructively co-dependent. Instead of treating others the way they want to be treated, many members of today's society treat *themselves* the way they want to be treated, and they only care about others in ways that further their own selfish ends. In other words they make themselves the star of their individual biopic and all the other people in their lives are, at best, supporting players and, at worst, extras in the epic movie that revolves around them.

At first glance, that sort of life has definite appeal. Who among us has not dreamed of being a movie icon, a rock star or a sports idol? But when you scratch the surface, many of those in the limelight have not found fulfillment in their money and fame.

Would you rather be rich or fulfilled? Would you rather be famous or have your self-respect?

I admit these are not always either-or choices. Certainly you can be rich and also be fulfilled. Yes, you can be famous and maintain your self-respect. But if you confront people around you with these choices many will opt for money at the expense of fulfillment and, as is obvious by a quick glance at YouTube, they will choose fame over self-respect any day of the week.

So with these choices in mind how, really, do you want to be treated? Do you want to be treated as a child who needs constant hand-holding and self-esteem-promotion to get through the day? Or do you want to be treated as an adult who can endure a disappointment, turn the other cheek at an affront and take a punch without collapsing to the floor?

One thing we all need is encouragement.

A friend and former boss of mine frequently uttered the telling phrase, "Life is hard. Then you die."

This double-dose of pessimism is the heart of many people's world view. They expect the worst and in what is, perhaps, a self-fulfilling prophecy, that's what they get.

As another former co-worker of mine frequently opined, "The difference between an optimist and a pessimist is the pessimist is better informed." To back up his premise, this friend, who happens to be the nicest guy in the world, searches the news each day for accounts of disasters, and then spreads the bad news far and wide to his many friends. Knowing I'm a sailor, he would deliver me maritime disaster stories on an almost daily basis, while another co-worker, a pilot, got the plane crash stories. He is not malicious. This is simply his world view.

The point of this is if you look for bad in the world, you will find it. If you look for shortfalls and tragedies in your own life, you will find them. If you look for shortcomings in your spouse, family and friends you will find them. So life is hard.

But the antidote to that hardness is encouragement. We all benefit from a pat on the back. We all enjoy a kind word or even a simple smile. Sometimes that is all it takes to shift your mood from negative to positive; it is all it takes to motivate you to move forward rather than wallowing in failure and self-pity.

Encouragement takes many forms, but many revolve around bestowing mercy — providing comfort that is unearned.

Most of us want to be treated with respect, with empathy, with sympathy, with understanding. We strive to be valued, listened to, understood, comforted, reassured, aided and abetted. We want to be part of a larger whole, be accepted for what we are. And at the same time in our heart of hearts we would like to be more than we are at this moment in time. We would like to gain greater respect, greater comfort, greater reassurance, greater peace of mind. We want to be independent yet not solitary, fulfilled yet challenged. And if we can make a positive difference in others' lives, most of us would achieve that fulfillment for which we constantly strive.

As I've mentioned before, this isn't a book about religion, but one does find endorsement for this conduct in the *Bible*. For example, Ephesians 4:29 intones, "Don't use foul or abusive language. Let everything you say be good and helpful, so that your words will be an encouragement to those who hear them." [New Living Translation]

By encouraging others through word and action you show them how much you value them for who they are. You will find it will make a world of difference to them and their attitude toward their lives. What you might be surprised about is the fact that it will also make a world of difference to you and your attitude toward life. Good deeds are infectious and the key symptom is improved happiness.

Chapter Four

Being nice is more than just nice

In spite of the existence and apparent success of those who do the opposite, there should be general agreement that treating others with respect, honesty and empathy is a good thing. If you are encouraging and empathetic, it will result in positive human relationships and a general betterment of one's life. Recent research even indicates that acts of giving trigger pleasure centers in the brain.

Treating the people in our personal lives the way we would prefer to be treated seems to be both widely practiced and generally acknowledged as logical and "right." In fact, if you ask people, many will tell you they behave and interact differently with their friends than they do with others. Often this involves treating those in their circle of friends with honesty and empathy — in other words treating them the way they'd like to be treated

— but that same level of deferential treatment does not extend to people they don't know or people they don't care about. While positive treatment of our friends largely seems natural, positive treatment of everyone we meet is far less prevalent. Individuals who would never dream of being rude to their friends are often routinely rude to "service personnel" like wait staff, airline ground personnel and retail salespeople.

So why is the GR Factor important to business success, you might ask. Doesn't success in business come from ignoring or denying the needs of others? Don't true riches come from exploiting others, not helping them? Isn't, in the infamous words of the fictitious Gordon Gecko, greed good?

What is amazing — and troubling — is that many self-professed Christians check their belief in the Golden Rule at the door each day when they walk into their place of business. I've heard more than one devout, church-goer say privately that when it comes to business "you do what you gotta do." I don't know exactly what they meant by that, but I don't believe it meant they were seeking deals that offered mutual benefit.

I once did some project work for an ambitious young self-professed Christian entrepreneur who was in the process of creating a number of related businesses. His first business was funded by an older businessman he had met in his church, but instead of using his efforts to grow that company for the benefit of both his partner and himself, the younger entrepreneur instead used the business to gain contacts and contracts that he kept hidden from his partner. When he felt comfortable going out of his own, he left the original business, which faltered without him, and his former partner, who had given him a generous start, was left holding the (empty) bag.

Certainly, this kind of tale will be familiar to those who 1. are wary of business and 2. are wary of self-declared "religious people." Many individuals who are not religious seem to have a sneering regard for those who say they are, and perhaps the above example is a good reason why.

A common outlook, especially in the halls of academia and in some political think tanks, is that business success is synonymous with greed, that businessmen really do believe greed is good. According to this line of thought, business is inherently exploitive. A businessman only wins if others – business competitors, consumers and the society at large – lose. But that view isn't just simplistic and myopic, it is demonstrably incorrect.

An analysis of enterprises that enjoy continuing business success demonstrates clearly that it is much more likely to be the result of positive outcomes for others than it is to be the result of an exploitative interaction (read "somebody getting screwed.") An important aspect of business success is sustainability. Real business success is not the result of One Big Deal in which the successful company vanquishes all comers in a pitched battle to obtain the Single Competitive Advantage.

Similarly, real business success is not a series of zero-sum win-lose situations in which one business continually bests others in a series of battles over a fixed amount of assets. Real business success is a sustainable, ongoing series of win-wins as part of an ever-growing creation of wealth. It is not about wresting wealth from others; it is much more about literally building wealth — assets, value, things — where there was little or nothing before.

Consider this simple example: The materials in a smartphone are of little value; the labor that is involved in the manufacturing of that smartphone is of little value; and even the accumulated and learned technology that enable the functionality of the smartphone is of relatively little value — individually. But when you put all those assets together — materials, labor and design — you have created substantial additional value where none had existed previously. That is wealth creation, and wealth creation is much more important to sustainable business success than wealth accumulation.

When you view business through that lens, it is not difficult to grasp that win-win transactions breed more such transactions and more growth. Win-lose situations, on the other hand, are restrictive of future growth.

"Why should I do that again?" the loser in a transaction asks himself. At the same time the winner will find fewer and fewer patsies to exploit, because word soon gets out that he (or his organization) is only interested in taking from those with whom he does business.

Does this imply that you should let competitors, customers and the general public "walk all over you?" Certainly not. But if you are unrelenting in employing the GR Factor in all your interactions with others, you will be able to build the ongoing series of win-wins that will sustain your business success.

Chapter Five

Integrity Builds Trust

One reason The GR Factor is so critical to real business success is that business depends upon trust. To maximize the success of the enterprise you need the trust of customers, of vendors and of your own employees. If you walk into a coffee shop, you are trusting that the premises are clean and sanitary, that the ingredients that go into your coffee are pure and that the employee who prepares the coffee knows how to make the drink you requested properly. When it comes to the transaction that buys you the coffee you trust that the proper amount will be charged to your credit card and the requisite bonus points, if applicable, will be added to your account. That's a lot of trust just to buy one cup of coffee, but it all works because the establishment is applying the GR Factor at every step along the way.

Multiply this by the billions of transactions and business agreements that take place every day, and you can readily see that our economy would seize up in paralytic shock if trust did not exist in the marketplace. In fact if a large portion of the populace suddenly lost faith in our monetary system, which relies almost wholly on trust, the world's economy as we know it would grind to a screeching halt.

Let me tell you a little parable about gaining and then losing trust. A couple of years ago, I was informed to the dismay of everyone in our household, that my middle daughter had been stopped by a local policeman because the left brake light of her older SUV was not functioning. This resulted in a "fix-it ticket." You prove you got the problem fixed, and the ticket is erased. So I was tasked with getting the brake light fixed.

Seeking a quick solution, I drove the vehicle to the nearest auto repair center, associated with a major tire brand, and told them the problem. The chief on duty immediately unscrewed the taillight lens, inserted a new bulb and replaced the lens. Total time: under five minutes from the moment I rolled in. I was happy the fix went so well and was so rapid, and of course I expected to pay for the service, but the technician said no. "It's just a simple thing," he told me. "No charge."

This is great, I thought, filing it away in my mind. Whenever I have a vehicle problem that needs repair, I'm going to bring it here. This man had treated me as I wanted to be treated — in fact a little better — and trust was established.

Over the course of the next two years, as our family had vehicle problems, I took the cars to this shop to be repaired. We bought sets of tires, had air conditioning repaired and a host of other vehicle maladies fixed to our satisfaction by this business. So trust had been established, and commerce — of benefit to both the business and my family — ensued. Nice little story with a happy ending if that was all there was to it, but then came the tale of the battery cables.

One day, my youngest daughter, who had inherited the

SUV from her older sister, called to say the vehicle wouldn't start when she got into it to drive home from high school. I called AAA, and I met the technician at the vehicle, and within a few minutes there was a new battery in the SUV, and my daughter drove it home. While this sounds like the end of the story, it was actually the beginning of a new chapter, because over the course of the next few weeks, the SUV would suddenly refuse to start. We then learned that after some manipulation of the battery terminals, it would regain the connection and start. With this knowledge in hand, I tightened both battery terminals, which were showing definite signs of age, and told myself to have them replaced. One more bout of non-start — this time while I was out of town and couldn't help — made me decide to have the battery cables and associated terminals replaced right away. So I took the vehicle to the local shop that had done all of our car repair work with the exception of the battery replacement. I told the service writer I wanted both battery cables replaced, and he said he would call me when he knew the price of the parts so I could officially okay the work.

I walked home, and over the course of the next several hours I heard nothing at all from the shop. Finally, I decided to call them to see what was going on, and the service writer who answered the phone said he wanted me to speak with Tom, the technician on the job, but that Tom was busy right then. I told him that I didn't know what Tom could want to talk with me about, since the repair I wanted was pretty straightforward, and he said he would go ahead with the replacement of the battery cables.

About a half hour later Tom called me, and he had quite a story to tell. He said that he had taken apart the SUV's brakes and found that it needed a brake replacement, front and rear. He also told me the SUV needed a wheel bearing re-pack, replacement of the upper steering control arm, and transmission fluid exchange. In all, the work he suggested that his shop would do on my daughter's vehicle would cost more than $1,700.

I'm certain that many people in my shoes would've bit the

bullet and told the shop to go ahead and do the work. But when it comes to cars, I'm not naive, having served as Editor of *Motor Trend* magazine and as Editorial Director of *Driving Today*. Further, my brother is a certified mechanic who ran his own independent vehicle repair shop for thirty-five years. And we both sensed that this laundry list of recommended repairs was far more than the vehicle required. (Unfortunately for me, he lives 1,500 miles away or he would be the one working on my cars.) So I said no to the additional and unneeded work, and Tom said he would "put it all back together again" and that I could pick our vehicle up.

I walked back into the shop about 30 minutes later to find the SUV waiting for me, but when I looked under the hood I found that the battery cables had not been replaced. Instead, the shop had taken the much easier step of clipping off the ends of the cables and bolting on new terminals.

So, as you can imagine, I have lost trust in this business, and I will never take another one of my vehicles there for service, tires or anything else. Now I have to find another shop to repair the family's vehicles when they need it, and that's a hassle, but the shop has lost a steady customer who over time would likely have brought it thousands of dollars of profitable business and provided hearty recommendations to others in the neighborhood. After initially following the example of the GR Factor, the shop in question did just the opposite, and by trying to cheat me by attempting to sell me repairs that were not necessary, it has instead cheated itself.

How do you gain and keep trust? By treating others the way you would like to be treated yourself. You must keep your word, deliver on promises, be on time and take responsibility for your actions and for your shortcomings. No one expects you to be perfect, but they can expect you to be real and to act with integrity.

Trust is critical to commerce, because if you don't trust those with whom you do business you are constantly playing defense in your business dealings. If you have the sense that those with whom you do business will treat you the way you want to be treated – with fairness and honesty – you don't need to spend nearly as much time in a defensive posture. Instead, your belief that those with whom you do business will actually do what they say they will do when they say they will do it enables you to be forward-looking and efficient. If your partners meet deadlines, provide agreed-upon quality, and stick to agreed-upon prices, you and your organization can spend much more precious time and effort serving customers and innovating for the benefit of customers. And that's as true if you are ordering a pizza as it is if you are buying an office building.

"Whenever I am afraid, I will trust in You." (Psalms 56:3)

Chapter Six

A Foundational Rule of Business

Treating others as you would want to be treated is not only a philosophy and an attitude, it is also the basic premise that enables win-win situations, and win-win situations are foundational to sustainable business success. Without the trust engendered by engaging in mutually beneficial exchanges, businesses would conduct never-ending warfare with one-another. They would act like feudal city-states, mounting rape-and-pillage raids versus their adversaries. And they would instinctively see all other companies as adversaries. This adversarial conduct might result in momentary gains, but those short-term gains will always be more than negated by the heavy costs engendered by such warfare.

Why? Because no matter how big your business territory is at some point you will run out of suckers to fleece and you'll exhaust all the naive to dupe. You can't grow an enduring customer base by exploitation. Word-of-mouth travels too fast. A much sounder course is to provide customers with real value – value they can grasp and appreciate. Those kind of customers come back. And tell their friends. The exploited tell their friends too, but they don't tell them what you would want to hear about your business.

You probably won't hear this taught in college business schools, but acceptance and adherence to the GR Factor – and the fact that the Golden Rule became an unofficial but nearly universal law of the land – is what made America the country of opportunity. Some revisionist historians claim that America's rise to prominence in the 19th and 20th centuries was the result of the abundance of resources, exploitation of labor, subjugation of native peoples and capitalist overreach. But that view is at odds with the facts.

Yes, America is blessed with an enormous wealth of natural resources. Yes, America possesses a vast and growing labor force that was and is poised to help turn those natural resources into useful products. But the same could have been said about imperial Russia or China in the 19th century. Further, Russia and China treated some native peoples within their boundaries with the same unfairness we showed Native Americans.

What made America different, and what made it the engine of global industrial growth, was the social norm of treating others as one desires to be treated, not just in personal affairs but in business. Far different from the stratified European culture most of the early American immigrants had abandoned, the American culture was (and is) one of equality. We are a society with the premise that no person is above another, that each person is entitled to equal dignity and respect in the pursuit of happiness. By its founding document, the Declaration of Independence, our society enshrined the idea of treating each other as we would want to be treated.

There are many sources of this notion of "do onto others." As we noted earlier, this rule of living is contained in the teachings of many of the world's great religions, and many secularist philosophers have also embraced this way of life. It came to America with its earliest European settlers as the "Great Commandment" springing from the teachings of Christ that all people, saint or sinner, are equal in the eyes of The Lord. And in the New World among immigrants looking for better lives away from static, closed societies that had sent them packing the basic tenet became not just a religious aphorism but also an American ethic. In fact one might call it the most American ethic of all.

In America those of all political stripes embrace the equality and sanctity of the individual as a basic truth, yet in other countries and cultures this is far from a given. Many other cultures, often influenced by their religion, enforce and even celebrate the stratification of society. Some groups within these societies are aided by the "system," typically a combination of religion and/or central government, to succeed, while others – often ethnic minorities, women, gays and lesbians – are discriminated against or actively persecuted.

This is certainly not to say that America or, should we say some Americans, have universally been kind, benevolent and supportive of women, minorities and gays or other groups or individuals. At many points in America's history quite the opposite has been true. We have both bad people and good people who, at times, act badly, as any society does. But that being said, this country has accepted and integrated immigrants from a variety of cultures on a broad scale unheard of in any previous culture. And as these immigrants have been assimilated, each has been imbued in the American way of life that includes the reverence for the sanctity of the individual, equality before the law, equality of opportunity and tolerance of others. Our Constitution both memorializes these values and gives them the force of law. In other words, through the Constitution, citizens are treated the way citizens would want to be treated.

Americans have earned a reputation as a people who are warm, friendly, giving and accepting of others. Americans of all political stripes decry intolerance and celebrate brotherhood. We admire charity and revel in our diversity while taking pride in the fact that we share basic human values. We are not a perfect people or a perfect nation, but more than most, we have endeavored to provide aid and comfort rather than conquest and subjugation. Why? Because a very American trait, inculcated across our society well beyond the reaches of our churches is the social norm of behaving toward others in a way we would like others to behave toward us.

Okay, so if you're an American you can pat yourself on the back. Part of our culture is to be giving and accepting. Part of our culture — perhaps the very best part of our culture — is the general acknowledgement of the Golden Rule. Sometimes each of us might forget that, and oftentimes it is much easier to accept others who are like us than those who are not, but this is an intrinsic truth about American society. It is a philosophy that has been and continues to be reinforced by our culture. "Love thy neighbor" is the way a very great many of us live our lives every day. It is not a coincidence that our biggest holiday is celebrated by giving presents to others.

Chapter Seven

Live Life Honorably

When you put the GR Factor to work in your business life, you will begin to see changes not only in how you feel about others but in how you feel about yourself. If you treat others the way you would like to be treated, many — yes, not all but many — of the people you encounter will respond in kind. If you give someone a smile and a friendly greeting, they will likely return that smile and greeting. In fact I invite you to do that today as you walk the halls in your office or as a new customer walks in the door. The response will be immediate and rewarding, and if you make it part of who you are it will change the way you think about others and, interestingly, the way you think about yourself.

If you treat people in an affirmative way behaviorists might say you are "managing interactions and reaping positive feedback from managing them successfully." A simpler way to look at it is by treating others the way you would like to be treated, in other words by putting the GR Factor to work in your life, you build your esteem in the eyes of others and, importantly, your own.

Treating others with honesty, decency and compassion has very clear positive effects on business results. Customers who are treated well are much more likely to return to buy again and to tell their friends and acquaintances about the good experience they had. Sadly, experiences like that seem to occur less and less frequently than they used to, so they stand out.

Similarly, co-workers and employees who are treated with honesty, decency and compassion by their supervisors most frequently respond by working harder and being more diligent in their tasks. Additionally, they will be more likely to incorporate the same positive traits in their interactions with co-workers, vendors and customers. As this expands from worker to worker, these kind of interactions "become part of the culture" and "contribute to organizational health," a important series of buzzwords in the boardrooms of many of our biggest corporations.

Incorporating the GR Factor can certainly be a strong contributor to the creation of a healthy organization, but I suggest you look at more than a "tactic" or "one tool in the toolbox." Instead, what I recommend quite emphatically is that you adopt the GR Factor as an intrinsic part of who you are not just because it works to win the respect, admiration and business of others, but more importantly because of the way it will manifest itself in your self-image. When the GR Factor becomes embedded in your way of life you will begin to respect and admire yourself more. And the value of that is immeasurable.

What I'm suggesting is that you live an honorable life. I understand that the term "honorable life" seems anachronistic and thoroughly old-fashioned, and in light of the individuals who gain fame and adulation these days perhaps it is. But that doesn't mean that living an honorable life is not a worthy goal.

Unfortunately, we live in a world of increasing moral ambiguity and relativism. This view takes the position that all religions are morally equivalent and equally valid, and it also postulates that having no religion and/or adopting an anti-religious stance is a valid moral position. Given this attitude's prevalence in the popular culture is it any wonder that many among decide they "will do what they have to do" and act in what they believe is their self-interest rather than treating others the way they want to be treated.

If all standards of behavior are equally valid, then there are no moral standards at all. Sadly, we see that manifest itself every day as people who are anything but honorable seem to gather esteem, riches and followers. In many ways our society seems to be in a rapid race to the bottom. If you want fame and fortune, do something that is crass, vulgar and deplorable. In fact, if you want continued fame, if you want to be seen as being on the leading-edge, don't do just one horrible thing but make saying and doing horrible, lewd, salacious things your signature.

When success is defined by your Insta followers, if your Tweet is "trending" and how highly your name ranks among search terms on the Web, it isn't difficult to understand why what used to be called "bad behavior" isn't simply tolerated; it is venerated. We have reached the global expression of bad behavior within a family, where any attention — even negative attention — is considered more desirable than getting no attention at all.

Sad as this is, contemporary society's norms, moral equivalency and the virtual absence of firm standards provides a gigantic opportunity for those who decide to adopt the GR Factor as their guiding principle of behavior and to live an honorable life. What is honorable, you might ask. I suggest you picture someone whom you believe lives life honorably. How would you describe their behavior? What characterizes their interactions with others?

I imagine that when you picture an honorable person you are thinking about a person who is honest, who keeps her word, who is humble, who is self-effacing and who constantly strives to help others in big ways and small. I submit to you that this is a person who has put the GR Factor to use as his or her moral compass.

People who live honorably are obviously beneficial to others. Treating others in the way they would like to be treated certainly aids those who are on the receiving end. But what might be less intuitive is that treating the others the way they would like to be treated benefits those who behave that way. They win the admiration of others, but, importantly, they can admire themselves, not in a prideful or boastful way. (Look what I've done for you!) But with the humble knowledge that they are doing the right thing.

There is a great deal of talk these days about self-esteem. Schools install programs to instill it. Non-profits, amateur sports associations and service organizations go to extreme lengths to avoid injuring it. But I suggest there is nothing so good as earned self-esteem. There is nothing more satisfying than self-esteem that comes from the achievement of living one's life honorably. In this case the giver is also the prime recipient.

"If you are wise and understand God's ways, prove it by living an honorable life, doing good works with the humility that comes from wisdom." (James 3:13 New Living Translation)

Chapter Eight

The Customer Is (Almost) Always Right

People are people. If you want to please customers, do what people like. This might seem like an utter no-brainer, but you see this commonsense notion violated at almost every turn. Rude waiters, indifferent store clerks, broken promises, long telephone hold times, baffling Internet-based "help" that does anything but really help – the examples are legion. Treating the customer the way the customer wants to be treated involves behavior that is just the opposite of the indifferent or downright antagonistic "service" we experience so often.

You know what you like, so it shouldn't be all that difficult to figure out what others will like. You don't have to hold an advanced degree in psychology to grasp what most of us want out of life. No, every person isn't like every other person, and we can be thankful for the variety. But people share many attributes, and several of those attributes revolve around the way they would prefer to be treated by others. Do you know any people who enjoy being treated rudely, being ignored or being lied to? We might not all like the same flavor of ice cream or have the same favorite color, but it is a pretty good bet that the vast majority of us want the same laundry list of things when we are in the role of customer or potential customer.

Let's unpack that a bit. Most of us want the same things, but what are those things? And how can you and your business deliver on those things? It is not enough to simply give the directive, even to yourself, that you will "serve the customer." How you go about serving the customer is of critical importance. Here are things you should do to bring the GR Factor to life in your business. I am reluctant to call this a "checklist," because a checklist might imply that you simply make an attempt at each of these behaviors and then check it off the list. Treating the customer as she or he wants to be treated takes more than a cursory one-and-done stab at each of these actions. You need to internalize it. In fact you need to live it.

Here are some actions you should take when a potential customer literally or figuratively (in the case of an online or phone interaction) walks into your business:

Greet them

A warm and sincere greeting goes a long way toward setting the tone for a pleasant, productive interaction. I give a practiced eye to "customer service" within a wide variety of enterprises — retailers, food service providers, hotels, online businesses — and it appears to me that the importance of an appropriate greeting is being recognized and acted upon more and more. For example, hotel housekeepers, who in the past would typically avoid any kind of interaction with guests as they pushed their carts through the hallways, are now actively offering a smile and a pleasant greeting. It is a nice change.

Human-to-human interaction when both people are in the

same place is easier to accomplish than it is online, but many Web sites now welcome you (or welcome you back if you have visited before and allow "cookies") with at least some kind of greeting. Online greetings can be tricky, because in many instances they appear to be a simulation of a sincere greeting...and a simulation of a sincere greeting is, almost by definition, insincere. As technology improves — and as Web-based enterprises realize the GR Factor is as critical online as it is in human-to-human interactions — a genuine greeting to a potential online customer will be better enabled and will grow in importance.

Acknowledge and respect them

A warm greeting is a good first step to acknowledging a customer. It is enjoying a comeback, but after that initial contact, the interaction between customer and service provider frequently comes off the rails. Why? Because it appears that many employees are instructed to greet but are not given any instruction at all on followup. It is like the high school kid looking for a date who has a good opening line — something like, "Hi, my name is (his name here)" — but has nothing to say in response to the reply. Sure, he's nervous, and there's some charm in that, but in day-to-day encounters with others the ability to communicate in a warm and friendly manner is an important step in establishing that you are there to help.

Tone is very important here. You as a customer or co-worker won't feel that you are being respected if the tenor of the conversation is cursory, superficial and dismissive. While admittedly you are not discussing Western philosophies or other weighty issues with your customer or co-worker, you should sound as if you are engaged and really care. The simplest way to do that — and by far the most effective — is to *be engaged and really care*. While it might seem just as effective to feign sincerity, it isn't. At some point others will grasp that you are insincere, and that will be worse than simply not caring about the communication in the first place. If you demonstrate you respect them, they will naturally believe that you are there to help them.

Listen to them
The first way you can help is by listening to them. Too often we are so eager to say what we want to say that we fail to hear the very clear clues that can help us understand and act on what others around us — including, importantly, customers — need and want. In the parlance of the day, we are so caught up in "delivering our messaging" that we completely miss the other person's "messaging." Why? We haven't learned, in fact we haven't even been taught, that listening is the most important part of communication. Look at it this way — you already know what you know, so you won't learn very much if anything by talking. But there is a very good chance that the person with whom you are speaking knows a lot of things you don't know, and the only way to learn those things is by "active listening."

Let me emphasize the phrase "active listening" here, because you might think it nearly amounts to an oxymoron. Most people characterize listening as being passive. One reason for that is that many don't pay much attention to the listening portion of the conversation, because they are so eager to begin hearing the sweet sound of their own voices again. You talk and then, as the other person talks, there is a lull until you begin to speak again. Brainwave studies have suggested that.

Oddly, this is especially true of many salespeople, because they feel internal pressure to make their sales pitch, and that pressure influences them to forego listening and concentrate on "message delivery." Ironically, that rush to get it all out there can backfire and deliver a message diametrically opposed to what they want to portray, namely, that they care about what the customer thinks and about what the customer wants.

If you are an active listener — if you pay close attention to what the person you are speaking with is actually saying — you will learn an enormous amount that can help you understand and serve the needs of that person. Some of what you learn will come from what they say and some will come from how they say it. Both are important...and valuable.

I have hosted a radio show for more than twenty years and over that time I have had the opportunity to see how much I talk versus how much my subjects talk while we're on the air. It is right there on the recorded audio "waveform" that is a pictorial view of the interview. What I have learned over time is in the best interviews my interviewee speaks three to five times more than I do. My job as interviewer is to draw them out and start them talking about a topic they know well. Then the listeners and I can learn the interesting things they have to say.

Now I'm not asking you to become a radio interviewer, but I am suggesting that one way to treat others the way you want to be treated is to "hear them out." Listen to what they have to say and respond based on the knowledge you gain from that. Don't be so eager to tell your story you never hear theirs.

Make them feel special

Actively listening to others is a very good first step on the path to realizing larger accomplishment — making others feel special. This is a very worthy goal, because in our day-to-day interactions with others, especially those we don't know or don't know well, we often feel lost in the crowd. When encountering a co-worker in the hallway or break room it is becoming more and more the norm simply to ignore the other person. No greeting, no hello, not even a smile. What can be more disrespectful and dismissive than that? But the promotion-seeking millennial middle-manager, who often appears to have been raised by wolves, will tell you, "I don't have time for small talk; I'm here to get things done."

My counter-argument is "if you don't have time for people, you are not a manager."

Ignoring a co-worker and missing the opportunity for positive engagement is problematic. Ignoring a potential customer and not serving her or his needs is downright idiotic, yet how often do you see that happen? You seek a sales associate in a big box store, and they try to appear too busy to speak to you. You walk up to the counter at your local pizza joint, and the clerk picks up the phone instead of saying hello to you. You try to use chat to get information on a Web site you're visiting for the first time, and you get nothing but a canned response telling how long the "wait time" is.

The upside of all these poor-quality interactions that run rampant is that it offers incredible opportunity for those who employ the GR Factor. People like to feel special. They like to have the sense they are being noticed and they count. One way to go about this is to learn their names and address them by name. For some this can be difficult, and I know this for a fact because it is difficult for me. Yet I know that when I make a genuine effort to learn and use individual's names, it can be done.

For more than a dozen years I coached softball teams in a local rec league, and that meant that as every season started I'd be confronted by the faces of about a dozen girls who were totally new to me. I did recognize my daughter and I did remember her name, but the others were blank slates to me. Still, as their coach, I realized that I had to demonstrate a personal interest in each of them individually as soon as I could. So I knew I had to learn their names — immediately. And after applying myself to this task, I discovered I could learn all their names and begin calling them by name during the first practice of the year.

Let me tell you, saying, "Molly, would you play a little deeper please?" is a lot better than yelling out, "Hey, second baseman, back up! Back up!"

On the other side of the coin, one of the reasons my favorite restaurants in town are my favorite restaurants is not the quality of the food so much as the owner of one and the bartender in the other know me by name. And I know Matt and Alex.

Make them feel "at home"

If you know people's names it is far easier to make them

feel comfortable and make them feel "at home." There are two hotels — one in Chicago and one on Maui — that my family and I patronize frequently. Why? The staffs of both hotels make us feel at home. There are scores of hotels in each locale, but we keep coming back to the same two hotels because we feel welcomed, acknowledged and comfortable. In fact, every time we check into the Maui hotel the greeter at the desk says, "Welcome home." I understand that they undoubtedly say that to all their guests, but it is appreciated nonetheless. Importantly, too, it is backed up by their attitudes and actions.

Digging a little deeper, let's explore what feeling at home means. Certainly, one nice thing about being at home is many of your questions are already answered. You know where stuff is; you know how to turn on the TV, hook up to wi-fi and where clean towels are. Your refrigerator and pantry have items you like to eat, and your clothes are hung up in your closet. Your dog or cat is there to offer you unconditional love (dog) or affectionate indifference (cat.) In other words, when you are at home things are both pleasant and simple for you. This implies that to make people feel at home when they are not at home, you must endeavor to make things pleasant and simple for them.

Anticipate what they want

How? It isn't all that easy, but a good start is by anticipating their needs before they can even be expressed. When they check into a hotel, they typically don't know where their room is or even how to get to the elevator, so make the effort to show them. When they order coffee in a restaurant, there is a good chance they'll want sugar, sweetener and cream, so provide it without requiring them to ask. When they are standing with a baffled look on their face at a self-checkout at the home improvement store, help them get the transaction started and walk them through it without demeaning their intelligence. Anticipating others' needs is a good use of empathy. If you try it, you'll like it.

Reassure them

Another way to make people feel at home is by reassuring them. As fragile human beings most of us need reassurance at almost every turn. We need to be reassured that we are loved, that we are noticed and that we matter. We need to be reassured that there will be food on the table, clothes on our backs and a roof over our heads. So anything you can do to reassure others by word and deed is a way of treating them the way they want to be treated.

Another wonderful thing about being at home is you are typically among people who give you the benefit of the doubt. Oh, I well understand that you can live in a home with a domineering spouse or a demanding child. But in most homes you can expect that others in your family will cut you some slack and put up with some of your idiosyncrasies and shortfalls simply because you are family. Wouldn't it be great if you received that same benefit of the doubt as a customer or co-worker? Wouldn't it be nice if others "had your back" even in mundane workaday situations?

Be real

Another luxury you have at home is you can "be real." Many of us build and maintain a facade when we venture out of the comfortable confines of our own home. The way we present ourselves to others is not how we see ourselves, is not who we are, but it is the who we feel others want or expect to see. That is as uncomfortable as wearing shoes that don't fit. So if you can offer reassurance to others that they can be themselves, that they can be real, you will be giving them — and you — a great gift. It is the gift of friendship, and each of us certainly enjoys being treated as a friend.

Offer comfort

One of the most heartwarming things friends can do for us

is offer comfort. Just as we need reassurance, we also need to be comforted. There are times when we face difficulties or even tragedies that can't be fixed. Instead, we simply have to endure them, and that is when comfort and support offered by friends is so very much appreciated. With any luck, your potential customers won't be coming to you expecting consolation and commiseration, but treating others with the kind of warmth you offer your friends will make a difference that you both will notice.

If you do these kinds of things for your customers, you will exceed their expectations, because, as I noted earlier, our expectations of customer service these days are very low. Many of us feel that if the transaction and accompanying interaction don't seriously irritate us, we are ahead of the game. But that is a pathetically low standard.

The good news is, if you beat that standard, if you apply the GR Factor to your interactions with others, you will immediately begin to win customers and friends.

No matter who you are, no matter how skilled, learned and brilliant you are, at some point, probably today, you're going to need some help. People (read customers and co-workers) like people who treat them the way they want to be treated. And they will reward that behavior by doing business with them. Wouldn't you?

Chapter Nine

Expect the Win-Win

It is all too easy to hear the GR Factor doctrine, nod knowingly and believe you are internalizing it, while you continuously fail to adhere to it minute-to-minute, day-to-day. The odds are good that as you read the previous chapter you agreed with much of what was being said. Yes, you probably said to yourself, I *should* make my customers feel at home; I *should* strive to have positive, fulfilling relationships with my co-workers; I *should* be real. But unless you make the effort to put the GR Factor into the center of who you are, unless you actively engage in the behaviors that were outlined in the previous chapter because you think they are the right thing to do, you will fall short.

Why? A big part is sheer laziness. In the short term it seems much easier to ignore the needs of others and care only for yourself. Back a century ago there used to be a popular saying: "A friend in need is a friend indeed." But in more recent times that homely call to help others has been supplanted by a new version that captures the values of the current era — "A friend in need is a pest." While this version of the phrase was originally a parody of the original proverb designed to be funny, in many circles it is now simply regarded as true. A friend who needs help is seen as a burden. After all, it takes a little effort to help your friend move to a new apartment, drive a buddy to the airport or take in your neighbors' mail when they are out of town. But aren't those things that you want others to do for you?

One aspect that might help to motivate you to put the GR Factor in motion in your life is the fact that helping another human being is a win-win. Now, when you are in the car driving your pal to the airport instead of watching March Madness basketball from the comfort of your couch, you might not think of that as a win-win. But unless your buddy is a complete jackass, he will appreciate your extra effort, and that will help cement your friendship. Beyond that, the most genuine win-win from the extra effort is the way it will make you feel about yourself. Unless you're a complete jackass — and I sincerely don't believe you are — helping a friend will confirm that you are a good person, worthy of esteem and worthy of love. The act of giving gives to the giver.

Okay, you've probably heard something similar to that before, maybe around Christmastime. You undoubtedly remember people saying it is far better to give than receive, a phrase the current culture — the "I-want-more" culture — has also turned on its head. "It is far better to receive than to give" is a phrase that might sum up much of our current culture's attitudes. But let me try to prove that it is better to give than receive with a story I don't think you can resist, because it is about a dog.

For years and years and years, my wonderful wife and lovely children had wanted a dog. And for years and years and years, I firmly resisted, not because I disliked dogs but simply because I thought having a dog would be a hassle. In my mind's eye, I pictured a dog would mess up the house, complicate our future vacation plans and lead to heartrending tragedy if it got sick or passed away. But the pro-dog forces in the house wore away at my resistance like the slow thawing of a glacier, and one day I relented. My wife and children told me they wanted to go to a pet adoption day, and I said okay.

So we went to the pet adoption, and that's where we met Austin. He was dirty-white, kind of bedraggled and thin and had a "kennel cough." Worse than that, he was a boy dog and my wife and daughters wanted a girl. But we took him for a quick walk on a leash, and we all fell head-over-heels in love with him. Over a quick lunch nearby, we decided we wanted to make him part of our family, so we returned to the pet adoption to make our intentions known. I thought we might be able to take him home with us then, but it didn't work that way. Instead, the wonderful woman who ran Rover Rescue, the pet adoption service, scheduled an inspection of our home.

It turned out the inspection and interview were very thorough. She questioned us about our lifestyles, and she made us assure her that we would feed Austin a healthy diet and not leave him alone for lengthy periods of time. She inspected our house and our yard to make certain that Austin would have room to roam while at the same time being unable to leave the yard on his own. She made certain our fences had proper latches and that none of our yard plants was toxic to dogs. It struck me that the inspection was far more detailed than anything I'd encountered in connection with having children. (Of course, there was no interview or inspection connected with child-bearing at all.)

The good news is that when all was said and done our household passed muster with her, and she agreed to let us adopt the wonderful mutt who has become one of the centers of our home. Technically, we "rescued" Austin, and it is obvious to each of us in the family that he is grateful. More than that, he is protective of us — always alerting us when a stranger is nearby — and he is loving to us. He shows us unmitigated joy when we walk into the house, and he spends a great deal of time near us, though he does have his own chair by the window in the living room. In theory, we have given a home and very likely an extended life to him, yet he gives us much more than he gets from us.

The day he was frightened by Fourth of July fireworks, ran away and couldn't be found was the saddest day in our family's history. And the next day when, after a great deal of prayer, he returned to us on his own, was a day of unbounded joy. Giving our home and our hearts to him has resulted in so much in return.

Okay, I realize that the typical human-to-human interaction is not always as pleasant as that rescue-dog story. While dogs seem quite capable of expressing unconditional love, many humans have a great deal of difficulty with that. And in their continued but largely unrequited quest for "fairness," people often look for reciprocity from every action they make. I did this for you, so you should do this for me. I scratched your back, now you scratch mine. It is as if they are seeking the human equivalent of Newton's third law of motion: "For every action, there is an equal and opposite reaction."

But that is not what the GR Factor espouses. The message is not "treat others as you would want to be treated *so they will treat you that way too*." The message is simply "treat others the way you would want to be treated." It is not expectations of reciprocal actions that are at the center. It is the inner sense you receive from helping others, behaving better than required, finding within you a higher self, that is the biggest reward. Others benefit when you employ the GR Factor in your life...but you benefit more.

If you don't believe it, I encourage you to put my notion to the test. In fact, I *challenge* you to put my notion to the test. Today.

For the next twenty-four hours, don't just give lip service to the idea of treating others the way you would like to be treated. Don't simply assume that you are making each interaction you have with others a win-win. Instead, be very intentional about it. Insist on it. Treat even the smallest sale, the most minimal interaction, as a opportunity for a mutually positive exchange. Even a simple hello can term into something much more profound. And valuable.

Do that for twenty-four hours. Yes, twenty-four hours. I swear it won't kill you. And then assess the results. Did others seem more responsive to you? Did you begin to forge relationships where you thought it was impossible before? Did you feel better about yourself?

In any line of business a lot of enterprises are selling essentially the same products and services. So while having great products is important; giving the customer a positive, fulfilling experience as they acquire those products and services is equally important. Of course in a service business the service is the product, so the quality of the service as measured by the quality of the interactions is paramount. Remember, when others win, you win.

Chapter Ten

Prepare for Challenges

The key to lasting success in business is treating others the way you would want to be treated. That is what this book is all about. But there is much more to it than a simple sentence, as the previous chapters have illustrated. To reap the most rewards, you must internalize the idea of treating others the way you would want to be treated, and <u>not</u> because you expect them to treat you the same way in return. Many of them will, but that is not nearly as important as the rewards you will accrue by going beyond yourself and living your life in an honorable way that provides service to others. Not only will you gain self-esteem, you will also gain a manner of living that removes doubt and streamlines your decision-making process. There is no need for long rumination over a big decision when the answer to the question is "do the right thing." Treat others as you want to be treated.

Understanding that is crucially important. Adopting the helpful, honorable stance as your persona gives you clarity about life. The fact that the clarity you obtain also positions you to win and retain the esteem of others is an important corresponding benefit.

But there is another side to this coin. You might believe that adopting the GR Factor as your mode of living makes you appear weak. In fact, you might resist treating others the way you'd want to be treated in your business, because you are afraid that if you did, you would be a "pushover." You fear that your competitors — and even your co-workers — would abuse you and your good nature. With this in mind, you might treat your friends as you would want to be treated, but you harden your heart and prepare to do battle when it comes to your competitors, suppliers, vendors and perhaps even your customers and co-workers.

In today's society in which many view interactions as "zero-sum" games in which there is a winner and a loser, a substantial percentage of the population seeks to exploit customers rather than serving them and to dominate co-workers and employees rather than collaborating with them. Many people who maintain warm friendships and family relationships allow themselves "to do what they have to do" when they are engaged in business or non-personal interactions.

To those of us who put the GR Factor in action in our lives, these people can present a significant challenge. I understand that, and I have encountered it myself. Along the way, some of my bosses, co-workers and even employees have taken advantage of the fact that I treat others the way I want to be treated. For instance, I don't engage in inter-company intrigue and political maneuvering. I don't expect or require my co-worker-employees to do things I wouldn't want to do. I don't lie.

To be frank with you, there are times that my stance on this seems to have injured my career, at least for short periods of time. But what I have discovered even when company politics have laid me low is, through everything, I have retained my self-respect. When I look in the mirror, I don't see a conniving worm who is only as good as his last back-stabbing. I see an honorable person whose integrity and virtue is widely respected. And that has immense value.

No one, except maybe another conniving worm, wants to work with a conniving worm. Since you can't trust them, it is hard to work with them, because you never know when they will throw you under the bus. Over time people shy away from associating with the office politicians, the back-stabbers and the self-serving twits. If one is installed as their boss, they dust off their resume and start looking around. If one is hired as a co-worker, they try to avoid contact and become defensive and wary. There is no doubt that these behaviors are symptoms of "poor organizational health." That means they are destructive to growth and progress.

Sad to say, but it is true that hacks, office politicians and "me-firsters" do win some inter-office battles. I am one of millions who have been their victims over the course of my career. But the fact is, if you internalize the GR Factor, if you live it day-to-day, you will not only survive but triumph in the long haul. You will be exactly the kind of person whom others want to work with, collaborate with and be around. Your light will shine, and success will find you.

There is more to this story, though. What I suggest is not — emphatically *not* — allowing yourself to be abused and victimized and expecting that, in the end, you will triumph over it. To the contrary, in the most strident terms I recommend that all who internalize the GR Factor, all who devote their lives to treating others the way they want to be treated, also treat *themselves* as they want to be treated.

This much-less-understood corollary of the GR Factor is of absolutely critical importance in achieving "Golden Rule" success in a business context. You should NOT "give, give, give, never take, always give." You don't expect others in your life to give eternally without ever being on the receiving end of kindness and nurturing. If you don't expect that of others, you should not expect it of yourself.

Treating others as you would want to be treated does not imply you must always give in, give up and bow down to others. It does not suggest that you should allow yourself to be used, abused or victimized. If you are a believer in the GR Factor, you abhor it when others are victimized. Certainly, you should not allow yourself to be placed in that same position.

Those who put the GR Factor to work in their lives can and should stand up for right, because they are in the right. They should not take license because they live their lives in an honorable way, but they can draw strength and resolve from their beliefs. In fact, treating others the way you want to be treated *demands* that you stand up against those who attempt to exploit your good nature or the rights of others.

Two principles should guide your behavior and your reactions to the behavior of others — what is fair and what is just? If you are like most of us (and are neither a sociopath nor a serial killer) you want to be treated with kindness, fairness and respect. It is of paramount importance that you treat yourself the same way.

Chapter Eleven

Who You Are Defines How You Treat Yourself

Many people who have a philosophy regarding their interactions with others don't have a philosophy or even a point of view on how to treat themselves. The fact is many people don't even have a well-defined self-image. They might have some vague notions about who they are — "I am a good person," "I fear failure," "I hope for the best" — but very few people are introspective about themselves. They can tell you intimate details about others and describe their characters to a "T," but they have never taken the time to figure out who they are and how they see themselves.

Some people are abusive of others; some are indifferent to others and some go out of their way to be kind, nurturing and benevolent to others. At the same time, many people don't even consider the fact that the decisions they make, the things they do and even the way they think influence their self-image and the way they treat themselves. They are too busy living their lives to pay much attention to the lives they are living.

Perhaps that is natural given the way we lead our lives these days. While many of us yearn for a "simpler life in simpler times," we typically don't act on that. Instead we do quite the opposite. Today's standard is to add continual complication in the form of more people, more activities and more stuff. This leaves little time for introspection.

Further, introspection isn't valued very much in this action-oriented, "do-it-and-pick-up-the-pieces-later" era. Instead of moving forward with care and genuine intention, the contemporary sequence of events is most often Ready, Fire, Aim. And you can make the case that "Aim" isn't really a consideration at all even after the fact.

Action is far more highly valued than contemplation. That is obvious just from the way we describe introspection. Look up synonyms for "introspective," and you'll find "inward-looking," "self-analyzing," "introverted," "brooding," and "navel-gazing." Do those terms have positive connotations these days?

One of the most important buzzwords of the past decade — almost more prevalent than "buzzword" itself — is "collaboration." Does a brooding, self-analyzing navel-gazer sound like someone you want to hang with? Does it sound like an ideal partner for collaboration? Since a great deal of value is placed on work groups and teams, those who often look inward and don't go along with the crowd are considered suspect. In a workaday world where results matter infinitely more than the way they are obtained, people who operate by a moral compass are seen as obstacles rather than assets.

While I heartily endorse collaboration in the right circumstances, it is important that *you* decide who you are and who you are going to be. Your North Star values should not be "crowd-sourced." Certainly, you can and should discuss your wishes, goals and aspirations with others on your journey of discovery, but the final decision on who you are and what you represent is yours alone.

Should you decide that the GR Factor should be foundational to the way you define yourself, that decision has implications about your standard of conduct. It means that you will make treating others the way you would want to be treated your core behavior. It requires that you be honest and caring. If you decide that honor, rectitude and concern for others will be central to who you are and how you comport yourself, you can expect to receive praise from some but, oddly, vilification from many others. Representative of the tenor of our times in which the cynical and self-serving are seen as smart, those who adopt the GR Factor as their mode of interacting with others are often regarded as naive, unsophisticated and old-fashioned. Perhaps hopelessly so.

Recently, I was in a session with a number of other executives from a wide variety of industries in a symposium on management, motivation and "personal marketing." In one of the exercises each of us was paired with another member of the group, and we were tasked with interviewing each other. One of the suggested questions was "What is your personal brand? What words describe who you are?"

To that question I replied, "Honesty and integrity. And I'm a person who tries to help others."

I thought my answer was both reasonable and unremarkable, but my partner in the exercise, who seemed like a perfectly nice guy, literally sneered back at me, "So mother, the flag and apple pie, right?" It was obvious that my answer had cost me esteem in his eyes.

To tell you the truth, his reaction and reply shocked me. And as a guy who has written about grisly crimes including murder committed by a former co-worker, I'm not easily shocked. I had difficulty then — and I have difficulty now — understanding why honesty, integrity and concern for others called for contempt and derision. Aren't these almost universally regarded as good things? Apparently not in the current corporate culture.

His answer to the same question gave me insight into that. While I said my brand was "honest and integrity," he said the words that best described him were his "ability to make very complicated financial issues seem simple." He further explained that he worked in the financial services industry, and his niche was writing newsletters and other business-to-consumer communications that made investment in his firm's products more appealing.

Now there is nothing wrong with that. Helping those who are unsophisticated in the world of investing to understand financial instruments better is a worthy occupation. As a communicator myself I gained empathy for him in that effort. But at the same time, I had difficulty determining how the ability to deliver understandable information regarding investments defined him. It also made me wonder if the information he assembled and disseminated could be trusted.

I have spent a significant portion of my life delivering what I believe to be useful information to readers, TV viewers and radio listeners. Much of that information is about vehicles and the vehicle-purchase process, while the balance has covered a wide range of subject matter from avoiding the flu to what really happened in a notorious crime. All of this, every bit of my output, is valuable primarily because its creator has integrity and reports honestly with the central purpose providing information that will help others.

So please excuse me if I disagree that honesty, integrity and helping others are arcane, old-fashioned and pathetically naive. My belief is that those attributes are of critical importance in defining an honorable person. Further, they are critical to the process of determining how we should treat ourselves.

If you can't trust yourself to do the right thing, then why should you expect others to do the right thing? You can't control others' behavior, but you should be able to control your own, including the way you treat yourself. Do it intentionally; don't let it just happen.

You must be intentional about the way you treat yourself and what you expect from yourself. By doing any less you let yourself down.

"He who walks uprightly, And works righteousness, And speaks the truth in his heart; He who does not backbite with his tongue, Nor does evil to his neighbor, Nor does he take up a reproach against his friend." *(Psalm 15:2-3)*

Chapter Twelve

Treat Yourself as You Would Be Treated

The way you treat yourself is critical to finding success in the GR Factor, and, at the same time, it is guided by the GR Factor. Since the way of life is centered on treating others as you would desire to be treated, it implies that you should treat yourself the way you would desire to be treated.

Though it might be counter-intuitive, often those who exhibit kindness and concern, love and mercy in their interactions with others are, at the same time, very hard on themselves. Some might say that their exhibitions of kindness are compensation for perceived shortfalls in their inner characters. But those who make the GR Factor central to their behavior need not worry about their character. They treat others well not because they feel bad about themselves, but instead because they feel so good about leading honorable, creditable lives.

Still, treating yourself as you would like others to treat you can be alien territory to many of us, often because we are unaware of how we treat ourselves. Even many who are very intentional in the manner they behave toward others have no philosophy when it comes to their own attitudes and actions. What do they allow themselves to do? What do they require themselves to do? How do they respond when their behavior does not live up to the standards they have set for themselves? These are all part-and-parcel of how you view your character. What must you be and how must you act to make the GR Factor central to the way you treat yourself? The following are some logical answers to

Be honest and truthful

One of the most important things we want from others is honesty. If those with whom we deal are not truthful, if their words cannot be trusted, we are forced to live in a never-never land of ferreting out the real truth from our interpretation of what others say. That is a very difficult way to live. Communication is slow, tortured and inexact.

Sadly, the tenor of the times does not highly value honesty and the truth. Honesty is often regarded as an arcane and anachronistic trait reserved for hicks who aren't smart enough to lie, and the truth is seen as malleable depending largely upon what can be obtained by slanting it, changing it or denying it altogether. In a society in which the self-serving end justifies virtually any means, the honest among us are often considered woefully out of date.

In the face of these headwinds, for you to achieve the peace of mind that putting the GR Factor to work can give you, you must be honest with yourself. You must try to see things as they are and see yourself as you are. While the truth about ourselves is among the hardest things for us to determine, we must make the effort. Painting too rosy a picture of yourself is delusional and destructive, and so is painting too bleak a picture of yourself. Try to focus yourself on the real.

If you want to learn about the "real" you, put on your thickest skin, be prepared to hear things you don't want to hear, and ask your spouse, your friends and your children to describe you. While possibly painful in the moment, it will be eye-opening. And it could well change not only the way you behave but also the way you perceive yourself.

Be honorable, earn self-respect

One of the key benefits of putting the GR Factor at the center of your life is that it gives you a consistently honorable way of conducting yourself. You don't need to alter your behavior to fit the circumstances or the audience. You simply need to do what you would like others to do in the same situation.

As this becomes central to you — as this becomes you — it will manifest itself in self-respect. You will treat yourself with honor and respect, because you earned it. By putting the GR Factor to work on your life, you need never be ashamed of your conduct because you will naturally behave in a principled manner. While this will win you friends and admirers wherever you go, its biggest benefit is the esteem it builds within you. You treat others well, and that behavior is constantly reinforced by those on the receiving end.

A more troubling result of putting the GR Factor into action in your life is it will also breed a few detractors. Typically the worldview of these detractors is so different from yours, so self-centered, that they can't comprehend why you don't lie, scheme and institute situational ethics to gain your own ends. That's what they do, so they think it is odd that you don't. Further, the very way you behave and the fruits that it brings you are an affront to them. In other words, good people have a tendency to piss bad people off. You will encounter this, but the self-respect you will build by behaving in a moral and ethical manner will enable you to overfly their ridicule.

Stand up for yourself

Treating yourself as you would have others treat you means that you believe in yourself and your principles and are not swayed by the popular culture. Just as you would take the side of another who was wronged, so you should take your own side if you are wronged. As an individual you don't innately deserve more rights and respect than others, but you certainly deserve no less.

Frankly this is an area of difficulty, a knife edge, and there is the potential to fall off on either side. While you deserve "the benefit of the doubt" as much as anyone, it is all-too-easy to slide from giving yourself benefit of the doubt to granting yourself license to behave selfishly. Additionally, since you are coming from the moral high ground, you might be inclined to give yourself permission to strike back in kind against someone who wronged you. As one who has decided to treat others as they would desire to be treated, you must resist that very human temptation for revenge.

On the other side of the coin, you might be so used to sublimating your interests in favor of others' interests that you enable some to take advantage of you. The fact you live your life by the GR Factor does not require you to be exploited or used. You would not sit still as others around you are taken advantage of, so you need to do the same for yourself.

In instances like this the GR Factor will lead you to the proper behavior by focusing you on what you would recommend another would do in your situation. Do you maintain your self-respect? Yes. Do you firmly maintain your position in the face of an unfair challenge? Yes. Do you stoop to dishonorable, vengeful behavior? No.

Those who treat others the way they want to be treated do not believe "an eye for and eye, a tooth for a tooth." Instead, they have faith their goodness will overcome the evil that has been done to them.

"Do not repay anyone evil for evil. Be careful to do what is right in the eyes of everyone. If it is possible, as far as it depends on you, live at peace with everyone. Do not take revenge, my dear friends, but leave room for God's wrath, for it is written: 'It is mine to avenge; I will repay,' says the Lord. On the contrary: 'If your enemy is hungry, feed him; if he is thirsty, give him something to drink.' In doing this, you will heap burning coals on his head. Do not be overcome by evil, but overcome evil with good." (Romans 12:17-21)

Respect your self-worth

You might expect a proponent of the GR Factor to be self-effacing and meek. Certainly, if you treat others the way you would like to be treated you would avoid braggadocious, boastful behavior. In this self-aggrandizing, self-congratulatory world, self-esteem is encouraged even in those who have little reason to have it. While each human being deserves respect for her or his humanity, the simple fact that a person draws in and expels air is not reason enough for them to claim elevated levels of self-esteem. Our world is filled with people who have delusions of grandeur and often delusions of adequacy. Today claiming credit far beyond one's accomplishments is a global epidemic. It is not what you have accomplished that counts; it is what you claim you have accomplished or will accomplish that gets attention.

A GR Factor-focused individual, on the other hand, deserves to respect her or his self-worth because they have earned that right. Just as you would naturally respect a person who behaves honorably and ethically, so you should respect that in yourself.

Make time for yourself

If you consistently act in a selfless manner, adhering to the goal of treating others as you would like to be treated, it is possible to lose yourself. You become so busy serving others that you constantly put your own needs and desires on the back burner. But you needn't and you shouldn't let that happen.

As a believer in the GR Factor you would advise others to avoid the trap of failing to recognize and act on their personal needs. So in the same manner you need to make time for those activities that are fulfilling to you. You won't do this in a licentious way, but some genuine "me time" is both therapeutic and well-deserved. Let yourself enjoy it.

Allow yourself victories and celebrations

In the same spirit, you should allow yourself to feel joy from your accomplishments. Behaving toward others in the manner the GR Factor suggests will reap you rewards in the form of appreciation from others. Be willing to accept that appreciation. Be willing to celebrate the minor day-to-day victories — maintaining your home, coaching a team, helping a neighbor — that are the things that make your life worthwhile.

Just because you commit yourself to helping others doesn't mean that you must put on a hair shirt and self-flagellate each day. You aren't simply allowed to have a good time; you have earned it.

Be merciful and forgiving

Those who follow the precepts of the GR Factor will notice a strange effect it has on their perception. After adopting the philosophy of extending their warmth and love to all they meet, they will not only gain rewards from it; they will also begin to wonder if they are doing enough. "Could I have been kinder?" they will ask themselves. "Could I have done more for that person?" "Were my actions misunderstood?"

This is both natural and healthy. It indicates a growing regard for the wants and needs of others. But it can also lead to self-doubt. And this is where you have to extend the same mercy and forgiveness to yourself that you would extend to others. If your actions are coming from the right place — a place of respect and love — then the errors that you might make along the way are forgivable.

You might say something in an effort to deliver a compliment that is taken the wrong way. Your attempt at a humorous comment goes awry. As long as these were meant with kindness, their failure is forgivable. Those who practice the GR Factor need not expect perfection from themselves, and they should treat themselves with mercy on those occasions when they are rudely reminded of their humanity. It creeps up on even the best of us.

Loving of yourself, not self-destructive

Those who adopt the GR Factor as their focus should not only be merciful to themselves; they should also be loving. Importantly, this means they must avoid self-destructive behavior. This includes things that are physically self-destructive — smoking, drug use, risky behavior — and it includes things that are psychologically self-destructive — abusive relationships, office politics, gossip, adultery.

Though at times we might doubt it, lying, cheating and stealing are not just bad behaviors; they are also self-destructive behaviors. We might get the impression that many who engage in those behaviors are advancing themselves by them, but we need to step back and consider how we measure that. Yes, liars might advance their careers in the short-term, but at what cost in relationships, credibility and self-respect?

If you follow the precepts of the GR Factor, you will always be able to look at yourself in the mirror and see an honorable person who is worthy of respect. You will not have the nagging conscience and pernicious self-doubts that plague those who behave dishonorably. That alone is reason enough to make the GR Factor your behavioral center.

Chapter Thirteen

Dealing with Anger & the Angry

Dealing with anger is inevitable in our lives. We live in an Angry Age, a time when multitudes feel free to vent their anger at others. Individuals lash out for real or imagined slights. Groups whose common attribute is anger believe that expressing that anger in gatherings of like-minded people makes them more virtuous. Perhaps the cause they espouse and the issue that has prompted their anger *is* virtuous. But what they miss is that by demonstrating their intolerance for those with views that differ from theirs, the anger they express is not constructive. It will not change minds. Instead it will prompt an equal and opposite reaction of anger from the other side.

Living in this imperfect world we call home, each of us has reason to feel anger at times. Injustice is always with us. The dishonorable appear to succeed. The innocent are frequently exploited. Life is not fair. (As we said in Chapter 3) The reasons to be angry are innumerable. But what does anger accomplish?

When you rationally consider the results of anger, what comes from an angry outburst or a heated argument, you will determine that far more often than not anger is destructive. In many cases you might have good cause to believe your objective is just and thus your anger is justified, but an unchecked expression of anger rarely helps achieve the desired result. Instead, anger is met with anger, and the situation deteriorates.

"Control your temper, for anger labels you a fool." So says the New Living Translation of Ecclesiastes 7:9. You can be in the right, but still be the fool if you allow anger and negative emotions to control your actions. Look back at your own life and count the times that good-decision-making came during moments when you were angry.

Some anger is caused by inadvertence. You accidentally bump into someone in a crowded subway car, and they get upset about it. Some anger is caused by disagreement on issues large and small. You believe your daughter should do X, and she thinks it would be better if she did Y. And some anger is caused simply because a chronically angry person is looking for a reason to vent his anger.

As one who makes the GR Factor central to the way you behave, you should remember the effective responses to anger will naturally flow from the desire to treat others as you would like to be treated. Despite the strong temptation to give in to anger, you must remember it is toxic to respond to anger with anger of your own. If you accidentally trigger anger in someone, you should accept the embarrassment and understand you would make the situation worse if you allowed yourself to become angry and express it in retaliation.

If you get angry over a disagreement, you need to take a second look at the other person's point of view. Perhaps your first perception of the issue is flawed. Perhaps the other person has a valid point. And even if they don't, getting angry with them over the disagreement will not solve the issue. Instead it will likely make it worse.

In the instance where anger surfaces because the person is perpetually angry, you must dig even deeper to use the GR Factor to guide your actions. Some people are inherently disagreeable. It seems to be their "natural state." But is it? Or are they angry because life has been unfair to them, because they have had to face hardships that others never had to face, because life has not been as easy for them as they perceive (perhaps correctly) that it has been for others. These people might provoke your anger, but they don't need your anger; they need your love. It is very likely portions of these people are broken, and they need love and mercy, not scorn. The correct response, as always, is to treat them as you would like to be treated.

This does not mean, however, that you drop your guard and enable the angry to hurt or take advantage of you. Angry people can be dangerous, both physically and emotionally. They can damage you, sometimes grievously, so in the spirit of treating yourself as you should according to the GR Factor, you need to set limits, and you need to be wary. Further, you don't need to weather another person's anger alone. You can enlist friends, family, neighbors, counselors and even law enforcement officers to aid you in situations where anger escalates and abuse becomes possible. This is of critical importance because angry people can be very dangerous people. Don't tempt fate by assuming you can fix a bad situation alone.

Angry people are often filled with self-doubts. Internally they question their own value, and often this leads to lashing out at others who they perceive are enjoying an easier, better life than they have. These people need our understanding and our compassion, but at the same time they can be treacherous. Their jealousy of others can induce them to sabotage relationships, torpedo business rivals and commit violent acts, all the while telling themselves they are justified since "everybody does it." Because they cannot be trusted, because their word means nothing, they are very difficult to deal with. They are dangerous physically and mentally.

The best recommendation is to stay away from angry people, unless you have the training and support to counsel and help them. As the Common English Version of Proverbs 22 says: "Don't befriend people controlled by anger; don't associate with hot-tempered people; otherwise, you will learn their ways and become trapped."

This last phrase — "otherwise you will learn their ways and become trapped" — is important, because angry, dishonorable behavior is a trap. You see others profit by duplicity, chicanery and office politics, and you will likely get angry at their perceived success. You might even be tempted to adopt their tactics, at least to counter those who are using them against you. That is the trap. If you do what they do, you become them.

Instead you need to exhibit patience and faith that treating others as you would like to be treated will bring to you success and happiness. It will. I guarantee that.

"Be silent before the Lord and wait expectantly for him; do not be agitated by one who prospers in his way, by the person who carries out evil plans.

"Refrain from anger and give up your rage; do not be agitated— it can only bring harm. For evildoers will be destroyed, but those who put their hope in the Lord will inherit the land." (Psalm 37:7-9 Christian Standard Bible)

Chapter Fourteen

The GR Factor as Owner

As a business owner you have the responsibility to set the tone for the entire business. You can do this overtly by constructing a Mission Statement and assembling a list of Values, and there is a great deal to be said for this approach. But many people who start their own business don't do that, and having started businesses myself I can understand why. Start-up mode confronts you with a complex maze of must-dos. The responsibilities are many, and the time to execute against those responsibilities is often too short. Because those "must-dos" really must be done if the new business is to have any chance of success, it is not difficult to grasp why a Mission Statement and associated Values declaration goes to the back-burner if, indeed, it ever gets on the stove in the first place.

What this means is the typical startup business has no expressed and agreed-upon philosophy. It has no code of conduct beyond what is legal in its state. It has no dispute-resolution procedure. And it does not explicitly tell its employees how they should act in regard to customers, to vendors and to each other. What very often happens in situations like these is the organization takes on the personality of the business owner.

There are some logical reasons this occurs. First, the business owner is very likely to hire people much like her or him, especially initially. Because of that, shared values are almost inevitable. Further, in the absence of a stated mission and commonly accepted written values, the employees of the enterprise will typically pattern their behavior after the behavior of the owner.

This can work well if the business owner has good values — in other words believes in treating others as she or he would prefer to be treated. The potential difficulty comes with the stress involved in a start-up. Again, there is much to do and not very much time to do it. The business is typically understaffed. The working hours are hideously long. Tempers grow short. Irritation builds. And all that takes a toll. Good values and honest communication are in danger of being short-circuited by the demands of time and by the necessity for quick fixes.

In the interest of moving the new business forward there is always the danger that the business owner "will check her values at the desk." She or he will put critical philosophies and values "on hold" while the heavy-lifting portion of the start-up takes place. In the pressure of the moment it could seem expedient — it could seem necessary — to turn one's back on one's values just to get the thing done.

"I'll just take this one shortcut," you might say to yourself. "It's not in my interest to tell the truth here, so I won't. But I'll never do that again."

You know the result of that: it doesn't just happen again. It happens again and again and again, and it becomes, ipso facto, the way the enterprise conducts itself. Because that is the way the business owner conducts himself or herself when doing business.

But you can't realize the immense benefits of the GR Factor if you try to turn it off and on like a light switch. And this holds true whether you are the owner of a business that is just getting off the ground or a long-established business with generations of success behind it. Many business owners are tempted to wear different personality masks depending upon whom they are talking to. For instance, they treat customers with incredible deference, while at the same time being hell-on-wheels with their vendors and employees.

In essence they try to employ the GR Factor in every encounter they have with a customer or potential customer, and they require their employees to act the same way. But because they have the power of the paycheck over their employees and the power of the purse over their vendors, they feel perfectly free to bully, intimidate and otherwise abuse them. Then they go home and lovingly kiss their wives or husbands, pet the dog and read nighttime stories to their children.

They subscribe to the theory that "Sincerity is the key to success; once you can fake sincerity, you have it made."

But it doesn't work that way, because people can sense whether you really care about them or if you are faking it. People can grasp if you are genuinely concerned about their welfare or if you are simply trying to appear that you do to further your own interests, not theirs. They might not catch on right away. That has certainly been the case in my life. But eventually they WILL catch on, because fakers will always betray themselves by putting themselves first in a crucial moment. They simply can't help themselves, because they are internally wired to view their interests as the most important interests. They will seem to be your loyal friend and supporter until they believe it is to their benefit to turn their back on you. And then they will gleefully shove you over the cliff.

The good news is that, over time, people will begin to understand that. Your actions forge your reputation, and those who turn in their friends and family for cash and valuable prizes will soon develop a reputation that will make others wary. In the final reckoning, they are shooting themselves not in the foot, but in the abdomen very near the heart.

The GR Factor is a powerful force IF YOU INTERNALIZE IT AND GENUINELY BELIEVE IT. If you don't internalize it, if you try to fake it, if you pay lip service to it but act in a different manner, you will never be able to realize its incredible benefits.

As a business owner you have many figurative mouths to feed and psyches to nurse. Certainly, treating your customers as they want to be treated is of critical importance, and many business owners quickly grasp that. But others don't. Others don't see the crucial importance of treating their prospective customers well. The ones who don't show their customers that they value them frequently find their businesses failing quickly.

But as a business owner you also have others within your sphere. If you are lucky you have employees, because their is only so much you can do and only so much money you can make as an individual. The typical business, whether it is a pizza joint or an Internet game-changer, wants and needs to capitalize on the multiplier-effect of having employees. This implies that to gain the untold benefits of the GR Factor you must instill it in your employees.

Let me ask you this: Do you believe your employees will exhibit the behavior you want toward customers if you don't model that behavior in how you treat them? Do you really believe that you can create a warm, nurturing environment for customers with a pissed-off, overworked and disgruntled group of employees and associates? When you were an employee in a previous job, did you like being bossed around? Did you work hard for a business owner when you thought he or she was abusing you and/or your coworkers? Because of complacency or laziness, do you let your employees get away with poor service delivered with a negative attitude?

Finally, and very importantly, does the atmosphere *you have created* in your business encourage the GR Factor? Or does it enable bad actors and poor servers to succeed?

My Dad ran his own small architectural firm for nearly fifty years. The firm had that longevity because it developed and nurtured long-term relationships with clients. Under my father's guidance, the firm treated each and every one of its clients in the spirit of the GR factor. This resonated with its customers, and whenever they had a task that might require architectural work or construction work, they turned to the firm. In essence, they were turning to the guy who did what he said he would do for the price he said he would do it. You could trust Nerad & Carlsen Architects because they internalized and acted upon the GR Factor in everything they did.

Importantly, this extended to the people who worked within the architectural firm. For most it was their "work home" where they were treated as well as they were in their own household, where they were valued, where they were respected, where they were acknowledged — every day. Many of them might have made more money working in a bigger, corporate architectural firm, but they stayed and became larger and larger assets, because they felt valued in ways that went far beyond a paycheck. Finally, when my Dad finally decided to retire at seventy or so, he had a ready successor — an employee who had joined the firm as a draftsman in his twenties and remained with the firm for thirty years.

When you own a business it is all on you. Businesses typically take on the personality of their principal executive. Employees see how the boss behaves, and that guides their behaviors. It is a giant responsibility, but it is also a massive opportunity. Don't blow it by saying one thing with your mouth and another thing with your actions. Don't try to fake sincerity. Live it!

Chapter Fifteen

The GR Factor as a CEO

If you run any company that is larger than a mom-and-pop-style organization, it is likely you won't have regular interaction with most of your employees. In fact, it is also very likely you will never even meet many of your employees. Because of this your ability to assure that the golden rule of business is being followed is exceedingly difficult. That is why "Corporate America" is widely criticized for its office politics, situational ethics and back-stabbing. In the absence of a well-understood, well-accepted and well-enforced code of conduct, the law of the jungle will ensue. If there is no policeman, who will keep the citizens from committing crimes?

Managing a big organization, especially one you don't own, is a stupendously difficult task, and I submit that the most important task is maintaining an atmosphere that promotes and rewards those who live by the GR Factor. The big difficulty in that is that large organizations, by their nature, enable and reward behavior that is in direct opposition to treating others as they want to be treated. In a substantial number of large organizations it is impossible to rise to the top without engaging — and winning — in office politics. The selfish not only survive; they thrive...to the detriment of the organization's goals.

Many of today's large organizations adopt high-minded mission statements and espouse laudable values. Yet individuals who get ahead in those same organizations often ignore or, worse yet, trample on the values the business supposedly champions. The hard-charging, take-no-prisoners manager is not just a cliche; it is the model of a successful executive in many companies. Concern for others goes right out the window in the never-ending quest to drive profits...or more precisely to appear to drive profits. Because those managers who bully their employees and co-workers and ignore customer service just might deliver increased revenues and profits *in the short-term.* But they are setting the stage for revenue decline and profit erosion over the longer term. The reason? You cannot continually exploit and abuse your workforce without doing dreadful damage to product quality and customer satisfaction. Put-upon, pissed-off, low-morale workers don't build great products and they don't deliver good customer service. Study after study demonstrates this. But many executives ignore it, because they are always looking for the quick home run, and they plan to be on to the next job before their abuses come home to roost.

Exploitative executives believe increases in productivity come from driving their employees to do more work for less pay. They believe that great customer service can be obtained by edict and enforcement rather than by nature and nurture. They believe the way to obtain rapid profit increases — and they are all about rapid profit increases — is by slashing costs, including personnel costs. The bigger the layoff the bigger the cost savings. And admittedly that gambit will frequently be followed by short-term profitability increases. But flushing away high-quality, productive staff members not only removes those staffers' contributions from the overall ability to deliver higher revenues, it also negatively affects the morale of those who survive the personnel cuts.

When employees see long-term, contributing co-workers put on the street, they immediately start to wonder about the security of their jobs. They also wonder about their desire to work for an employer that seems to care so little for its employees...like them. Some of those wondering workers — often the most productive of them — find other opportunities and leave the company. Those who stay are perpetually waiting for the next big boot to drop. You can bet those employees will not be motivated to assemble great products or deliver great service.

You might assume that Human Resources departments, in an effort to protect and promote the values the organization claims to live by, would be a bastion of good behavior that respects the rights of the individual worker. But instead, HR departments are among the most exploitative of all, treating individuals as a commodity and making dollars-and-cents decisions that do not take into account their victims' humanity. Too often layoffs of hundreds or even thousands of workers who contributed their loyalty and labor to the organization are treated in the same way as closing out and selling off a poor-selling line of goods.

People are not stuff. Every individual who contributes to the organization should be treated with honesty, empathy and respect. The Values statements of many large organizations promote these ideas. But you have to wonder how many big organizations really "walk the talk."

Here are some symptoms that characterize organizations that don't make the GR Factor central to their operations:

1. Office politics and "the rumor mill" run rampant
2. Some are promoted despite poor performance
3. Some promotions stymied despite good performance

4. Employee turnover is frequent
5. Morale is a perpetual problem
6. Product quality is in decline
7. Customer service is in decline
8. Innovation is infrequent
9. Departments are "territorial" and uncooperative
10. Business results (revenucs and profits) are declining (things generally suck)

Those of us who have been in the workforce for any length of time have labored (and I do mean *labored)* in organizations that have those characteristics. In many instances the CEO talks a good game about "honest and open communication" and "rewarding good performance," but what employees see is those who engage in backroom politics and bluster get promoted, while those who contribute without engaging in brown-nosing and rumor-mongering get passed over or laid off. A key reason this occurs is the CEO, who might have landed his job through office politics and short-term performance, doesn't really believe in and certainly doesn't live the GR Factor. Some business experts might tell you a CEO of a major corporation cannot afford to treat others as she or he would like to be treated.

I would claim quite the opposite. In an era when "organizational health" is a hot topic, when "poor organizational health" is the primary symptom of a corporation in trouble, a forward-thinking, profit-seeking CEO must put the GR Factor front and center. If the corporation fails to make the customer feel valued by providing that customer with superior products and superior service, the corporation will lose market share, revenues and profits to competitors who accomplish those fundamentals. And the very best way to accomplish those fundamentals is by making the GR Factor central to the way the company conducts itself with customers, employees, vendors, community members and the world at large.

It might appear that an effort to change an organization whose personality has been forged by the nexus of inertia, political intrigue and territorialism into a bastion of the GR Factor is a nearly impossible task. But the good news on that score it is far easier to put a company on a path of empathic and ethical behavior than you might anticipate. The reason? That is the kind of organization in which most people want to work.

Employees really want to like, respect and look up to their boss. They want to be treated with kindness, mercy and understanding. They want to be trusted with responsibility and to be expected to do the right thing for customers. Further, customers, vendors, the community and the world will heartily reinforce these behaviors. Why? Because those behaviors are good for them.

So the CEO has a giant opportunity right in front of her or him. The CEO can embrace and enforce good values exemplified by the GR Factor, and reap the rewards that come from that. The rewards are many:

1. High morale
2. Low turnover
3. Strong ability to attract talent
4. Great customer service
5. High-quality product offerings
6. Segment-leading innovation
7. Strong inter-departmental cooperation
8. Improved business results (Things don't suck)

Yes, there will be some difficult days as the organization transitions from an atmosphere of Machiavellian intrigue to one of nurture, care and mutual support. You can be the model of this behavior with your own direct reports. You can demonstrate this behavior in large-group meetings and even sing its praises at all-company Town Halls. You can even bring me in to give a presentation about it. But all of these good intentions can go off the rails if your direct reports and middle managers don't buy in and model this behavior as well.

My recommendation might at first glance seem contradictory, but you must be relentless and insistent on doing good. You must be intolerant of the intolerable. Those who don't buy into the GR Factor can be incredibly antagonistic toward those who do. You can't let toxic employees taint the medicine. The thing they say about one bad apple is true. As you institute the GR Factor as your organization's North Star, some of the office politicians will scoff and then bail. Those who don't change their ways should be encouraged to leave, because those who simply pay lip service to treating others as they would like to be treated will make it very difficult for the organization to act that way.

You might well fear that you are going to lose top leaders, and that your business results will suffer because of it. But you will immediately find that those supposed "hard-chargers" who you thought were driving the business were actually driving customers ad co-workers away. One thing that is reliably true about selfish people is that they are consistently selfish in everything they do. If they will lie to others, they will lie to you. If they will cheat others, they will cheat you. Your organization is better off without them.

Chapter Sixteen

The GR Factor as a Middle Manager

The previous two chapters described how and why the GR Factor can and should be instituted in a business organization by executives (owner or CEO) with the power and influence to effectuate that. But for a middle manager, adopting and instituting the GR Factor can be more difficult, especially in an organization that either doesn't emphasize such behavior or, even worse, actively engages in a different course that involves some degree of customer, vendor and employee indifference or even abuse.

Of course, if you find yourself in such a company, your best course is to exit and seek employment with a company whose philosophy and business practices emphasize treating others well or, at the very least, is agnostic on the issue. While it is possible to soldier forward in GR Factor style within a company that doesn't have those values, it takes a high degree of patience, effort and capacity for accepting ridicule. And you'll have a difficult time turning the ship if you can't get your hands on the wheel. In many instances, despite your best intentions, it might just be a losing battle, especially if the company is, by its actions, antagonistic toward its employees and customers.

But if the company is essentially agnostic on the GR Factor — it doesn't espouse it but it doesn't actively oppose it — there is the strong possibility that the success that comes your way by treating others properly will get noticed and lead to promotion and additional responsibility. In that way you can spread the seeds of the GR Factor in larger and larger fields.

If you have reasonable flexibility as a manager you will be able to institute your philosophy in your area of responsibility. It might be a department, a work team or a shift, but for any group in which you have hiring-and-firing authority and some latitude in managerial style you can use the GR Factor to improve performance. If you model GR behavior, make hiring decisions based on employing others who share this world view and you instill this philosophy as desirable in all your employees, you will soon discover that you will have one of the best-performing, most productive departments in your org. It will enjoy high morale, have little turnover and create satisfied customers. Your area of influence will be among the most productive and cost-effective in your organization, and your hard-driving, nit-picking, micro-complaining fellow managers will wonder how you do it. Some will say that your team members are really responsible for the success, and that you are just riding a wave. Others will simply ascribe it to dumb luck. In reality it is neither dumb nor luck.

What many don't grasp is the GR Factor is a motivational tool, perhaps the strongest motivational tool you can have in your arsenal as a middle manager. I know this firsthand because I have spent most of my career as a middle manager in a variety of organizations from global automobile manufacturing and marketing companies with thousands of employees to boutique public relations agencies with just a handful of co-workers. In each instance, the managerial style of treating people as they would want to be treated resulted in improved performance, higher morale and better retention of key employees. When you think about it, that is nothing but logical, right?

Top-quality workers want to function in an environment in which they are respected, honored, and rewarded for their achievements. They want to work in a place where they are treated like the professionals they are, so giving them "supervised autonomy" is important. As a manager you do not — you cannot — let your employees do anything they want. Humans are too fragile and too impetuous to allow that. But you must direct with loose reins and enable the creativity and ambition of your employees to come into play. This management style will create outcomes better than you could have imagined.

Of course, these suggestions are blasphemy to "command-and-control" managers who attempt to motivate by fear and bluster, who respect no opinions other than their own and who drive their best workers out of the company and onto the employment rolls of their archest competitors. I have worked under c-n-c managers and worked side-by-side as peers with others, and it is a painful and very unproductive experience.

What they fail to grasp is the elemental fact that employees are human beings. As *human* beings — and I emphasize the word "human" very intentionally — they all want to do what humans through history have done, namely, exercise their free will. In my more than forty years as a manager of operations large and small I have come to realize that people want to do what they want to do. As a manager you can try to thwart that, you can try to force the proverbial square peg into the round hole. Or you can take the much more effective approach of making the things that you want your customers, employees and co-workers to do into *things they want to do*. The absolutely most effective way to do this is by making the GR Factor central to the way you manage and, most importantly, to the way you behave.

"Well, how does that work?" I can hear you asking. "Yes, treating employees as they would like to be treated probably makes them feel good. But how does it motivate them to do the work that needs to be done? How does it motivate them to do objectionable work like cleaning toilets, scraping barnacles or trying to calm down an irate customer?"

Here's the answer: The GR Factor motivates employees to do all manner of difficult, onerous, repetitive and boring tasks because *it respects and rewards their basic humanity.* A manager who lives the GR Factor honors them, supports them and has their back. In unconscious recognition of that, employees will perform all manners of jobs, duties, chores, assignments and missions. They will do them willingly and without question, because they so highly value the fact that their basic humanity is being respected.

Command-and-control managers don't do that. They can't do that. They don't even imagine that can be done. Their only motivational tools — bluster, anger, threat of firing — are barely motivational tools at all. In fact, many who study effective management would call them "de-motivational." Threats and intimidation actually prompt behavior that is the exact opposite of what the c-n-c managers are attempting to accomplish. For example, I'll never forget the story about the workers in Jeep's Toledo, Ohio, plant who got so angry at their oppressive managers that after building each Jeep on the assembly line *they welded the doors shut.* If you want to see passive aggressive behavior, just watch the behavior of employees with a command-and-control boss.

Take note, too, this is not speculation. These are not the idle musings of an ivory tower theorist who has never managed a lemonade stand. In my own very lengthy managerial career that started when I became the Sports Editor of three newspapers at the age of 21, these tenets have been proven over and over and over. They were forged by the intersection of my religious and ethical beliefs and the knowledge I gained as a Management

Major in the well-respected business school of a major university. And they have been honed and distilled through many decades of a successful management career in various businesses.

Here is an example. In my mid-thirties I managed to get a job as a writer at one of the top three auto enthusiast magazines in the country. As lowest man on the editorial department totem pole, my first "office" was a desk in the "coffee room." While it lacked privacy, it did give me great opportunities for interaction with other staff members as they got their coffee or pulled their lunch bag out of the refrigerator.

Little more than a year into my tenure at the magazine, the top executives of the publishing company decided to fire the Editor of the magazine. It was a ritual they conducted every few years. (I would later refer to the Editorship there as "an exit-level position.") Interestingly, they canned the Editor, but they had no idea who would replace him. Odd, but emblematic of how the company was being operated — command-and-control in the extreme.

The good news for the company was that I, the low man in the coffee room, knew how to run a magazine. By that time I had already served as the Editor-in-Chief of two national trade magazines. So I understood what needed to be done and I had the management chops to do them. With no change in title and no more authority than what the individuals on the staff would grant to me, I began functioning as the Editor of the magazine. With the Managing Editor and the complete cooperation of the editorial team members, I planned every issue, edited every bit of copy and assigned every story. Again, I was just a few months away from being "the new guy in the coffee room," but I was able to lead this highly professional team *because they knew I respected and valued them*. Good things began to happen.

The magazine went to the printer on time every month avoiding last-minute rush charges. The well-conceived monthly issues that featured compelling cover photos and intriguing cover blurbs sold well on the newsstand. Staff members began to develop a strong esprit de corps. Cooperation with other departments, like circulation and sales, grew much more vibrant as the rising tide lifted all boats.

Within a year our magazine, which was a distant number three in newsstand sales when I joined it, had become the best-selling auto enthusiast title in the country. And it stayed that way for my entire tenure there.

Along the way I finally got the title of Editor to reflect what I had been doing for a couple of years. We added some very talented staff members who enjoyed the new open, creative atmosphere. The magazine got better and better, because each and every member of the staff felt an ownership of its success. Liberal use of the GR Factor enabled each team member to feel respected, valued and important. And they worked very hard to retain that feeling.

I know for a fact the GR Factor works. It is the best tool a manager can wield. And it will bring results. The only caution I would make is you can't fake it. You can't pretend your way into the success treating others well will offer you. You must live it. You must be it.

Chapter Seventeen

The GR Factor as a Single Contributor

In many ways using the GR Factor as your North Star as an employee with no management responsibilities is an easier task than it is for a middle manager or for a new CEO who is inheriting a company culture that doesn't have GR in its DNA. Since you don't supervise anyone — you are not a boss — no one in your organization will expect you "to act like a boss." You don't have to assume a tough, authoritative demeanor to impress your supervisor and/or the owner of the company that you "mean business." If you treat others — customers, co-workers and your superiors — the way you'd like to be treated, you will be viewed as a model employee.

Sure, an annoying co-worker might bug you. Sure, some customers will strain your patience. Sure, an uncaring, unfeeling or downright pernicious boss will test your resolve. But many a toxic boss is happy to have an employee "who has a way with customers." And if you treat your boss as you would want to be treated, she or he will quickly become your fan. In fact, your boss will begin to wish that all her or his employees were just like you.

When you are what is now commonly referred to as a "single contributor" — an employee with no supervisory responsibilities — your key interactions will be with your immediate boss/supervisor and your co-workers. If you are in a customer-facing position you will, of course, interact with them as well.

The GR Factor has implications for each of those interactions. With customers, the GR Factor is very clear. Treat them as you would desire to be treated as a customer yourself. You will also discover if you begin to treat co-workers and your supervisor like your customers, it will deliver exceptionally positive results. Some of this was discussed in Chapter 7, but using the GR Factor as your default in *every interaction* is the key. These important points that facilitate that bear further exploration. Remember these are not "check-the-boxes" suggestions; these are recommendations for living your life.

Greet them

You want to get off on the right foot with every customer, and the best way to do that is through a warm and sincere greeting. People want to be acknowledged, and customers typically expect more acknowledgement than a person you encounter on the street based on the fact they expect to give you their business. Ignoring them by delaying the greeting can quickly send the opportunity for a positive interaction right out the door. It might send the prospective customer right out the door, too.

Acknowledge and respect them

A warm greeting gives the customer hope that her or his expectations will be fulfilled, but all of that will come crashing down if there is no follow up. After the greeting, seek out the reason the customer came in. What do they need? How can you be of service in making that happen for them? Some customers are genuinely "just looking." That's cool, and it is no reason for you to immediately dismiss them, yet as customers we have seen that behavior over and over. You say, "Thanks, I'm just looking" and you suddenly become invisible…or worse. If a potential customer is in your place of business, she or he deserves your respect. Of course, your supervisor and-workers deserve equivalent portions of respect.

Listen to them

Frequently we are so eager to say or do something that we fail to hear what the potential customer says he or she wants. The lack of communication can be a critical "fail-point" that can send the dialogue in a negative direction. Listening is not a well-taught skill, yet listening is the most important part of communication. And it is of critical importance in positive customer interaction. If you pay close attention to what customers say, you will learn an enormous amount that can help you serve them.

Make them feel special

The GR Factor can be of immense benefit in making the customer feel special, because the tone and emotions expressed are genuine. We all have been "glad-handed" and felt dismissed but someone who said all the right words but did not say them in a meaningful way. If you live the GR Factor you will make others truly feel special. The interaction will be consequential because the nice things you express *you actually mean*.

Learn and use their name

A great way to signal to people that you acknowledge and care about them is to call them by name. I know this can be difficult because there is always the fear that you will get their name wrong and be embarrassed. I absolutely have that fear myself, and I have stumbled over this piece of my own advice because of it. Yet with a little effort you can learn and use individual's names, and when you do the light will always go on.

Make them feel "at home"

One of the best things about being at home is many of your questions are already answered. You know where stuff is and you know how things work. You are "in your element" and your comfort level is high. To enable people feel at home when they are in your business, you must make things pleasant and comfortable for them.

Anticipate what they want

You can get a head start on making them feel at home by anticipating their needs before they can even be expressed. The vast majority of your customers will have similar questions and similar desires. Identify those questions and answer them before they are asked. (Note, this also is a great way to deal with your boss.)

Give "the benefit of the doubt"

When you are at home others in your family cut you some slack and put up with your idiosyncrasies and missteps because, after all, you are family. In a business setting, customers, co-workers and even supervisors would dearly love to have that same feeling of being accepted, but they rarely get it. If they work in a command-and-control workplace where corporate politics trumps all, they must constantly watch their backs. Workers in a GR-oriented business, on the other hand, have each other's backs. They can be trusted not to bury the dagger in yours.

Be real

In many of our daily interactions, especially in the workplace, we hide behind a facade. We build a "work personality," and that's the person we are during our working hours. But often that is a very confining space. If in your interactions you enable others to be themselves rather than playing the work part, you liberate them. This does not mean that you make every one of your conversations start with politics and end with religion, but if you treat others as you'd like to be treated, being real can also be safe.

Offer comfort

There are times when personal difficulties and tragedies slide into the workplace. That is to be expected because your customers and co-workers are human beings. Stuff happens, and at times people need to be comforted more than they need anything else. Again, if you live the GR Factor, offering comfort and giving encouragement will be second nature to you, because empathy is part of who you are.

What can be troubling is the fact that even if all of the above become second-nature to you, even if you sincerely live your life with the goal of making life better for others, you might still be confronted — or back-bitten — by a detractor or two. Some will call you fake. Some will claim you are "not really as good as you think you are." Some will simply envy the relationships you make and maintain.

This can be frustrating, but it is a part of living the GR Factor. Some don't get it, and, sadly, they probably never will. These are the people who really test your resolve and your commitment to GR. It can be tempting to strike back at them, to relax your belief in treating others as you want to be treated because their actions indicate to you *they don't deserve to be treated that way*. The temptation to strike back is a natural one in those circumstances, but resist it, resist it with all your strength. Because if you strike back, if you respond to them in the same way that they behave toward you, you become one of them.

As I said before, you can't turn on the GR Factor as if it were a light switch and then turn it off when you feel you don't need it. It just doesn't work that way. If you adopt the GR Factor as your way of life, you must live it. You can't just flick it on when you think it'll do you some good. They have a name — actually a psychological label — for people like that. They are called sociopaths. The sociopathic lifestyle might offer a high level of excitement but it is not something I'd suggest.

I have met several sociopaths in my time, including a convicted murderer about whom I wrote a book. Their lives are often colorful but ultimately tragically self-defeating.

Chapter Eighteen

The GR Factor as a Supplier/Vendor

Those who work from a supplier or vendor often find themselves in a difficult position. Sometimes their task is simply to supply customers with goods or services, but at other times it becomes far more complicated than that. Often a vendor has significant influence on the success or failure of another company. For instance, it can be an integral part of its customer's supply chain. If it fails in that responsibility, the customer-company suffers as much — and sometimes even more — than the supplier does.

A vendor might also represent the customer to the outside world. Advertising agencies, public relations agencies and social media counselors are often granted the responsibility of creating and maintaining the public face of a brand. Missteps in that effort can have dire consequences for the client. We have all seen instances in which an advertising agency engaged a spokesperson for its client only to discover later that the spokesperson was involved in drug abuse, pedophilia, sexual misconduct or murder. Sometimes the agency gets fired, but that doesn't undo the damage caused to the client, damage that can extend for years.

Even when you as a vendor do everything right, it is possible that the client will blame you for problems that arise, even if you had no authority to head off those problems. Vendors and suppliers get used to being assigned the most onerous tasks and routinely being the scapegoat for clients' shortfalls. It comes with the territory. The client has "the power of the purse," and most clients are quite willing to wield it. If you ever wanted to know what a punching bag feels like take a job with a vendor.

Suffice it to say, being a supplier is always a challenging position. Rather than dwelling on the negatives, which I've done a good job of, it is more productive to look at ways to make a vendor/supplier role fulfilling and successful. And I expect you know what I'm going to suggest — the challenges of being a supplier respond very well to the application of the principle "treat others the way you want to be treated." If you live the GR Factor as a supplier/vendor you will find your relationships with your customers will improve markedly.

As a vendor you have customer companies with the same needs, desires and expectations as other customers. But in many instances you have to face the fact that many a customer company that prides itself on delivering great customer service for consumers has no compunction at all about grinding its suppliers. Going in, vendors can expect to face constant price pressure, ever-expanding responsibilities without commensurate compensation and the ongoing reality that they can be replaced at any time for any reason or no reason at all. If it sounds like walking a tightrope without a balance pole, you are not off the mark.

At the same time, while vendors and suppliers are frequently beaten up by their customers, the vendor-customer relationship is a two-way street that is filled with potholes on both sides of the median. While companies often abuse their suppliers, vendors often supply poorer quality goods than promised, deliver them late and ignore attempts at communication that might improve the situation. Often suppliers and vendors try to "explain away" poor quality products and service rather than getting to the root cause of the shortfalls. If you don't address the cause of the disease, papering over the symptoms will be a short-term fix at best.

Happily, as you make the GR Factor your way of living you will find it especially helpful in relationships with clients and client companies. I use the term relationship intentionally, because agency-client or vendor-client interaction has much in common with a long-term personal relationship. Both parties enter the relationship with high expectations and both want it to last. But as they say, "familiarity breeds contempt."

Like a bad personal relationship, a supplier-client relationship can deteriorate for a number of reasons — neglect, laziness, taking the relationship for granted. If you insist on making the GR Factor central to the relationship, you can avoid those problems. You don't like being neglected, do you? You don't want to be thought of as lazy, do you? And you don't want your relationships with others to be taken for granted, do you? So it is clear that if you treat your client/customer-company as you would like to be treated you can head these problems off at the pass.

For a portion of my career I managed the public relations activities of an Asian-based global automaker for a well-respected, multi-national public relations agency. The pressures on everyone involved were enormous. The carmaker was being squeezed by larger competitors and had financial problems. Because of that, it was under-staffed and the employees were over-worked. Rumors floated that the company was about to be acquired by a much-larger competitor or that it was going to be liquidated. Needless to say, it wasn't the most pleasant place to work.

Yet for the agency, the carmaker's public relations business was of crucial importance. As one of the ten biggest accounts in the agency's worldwide portfolio, the auto company business went a long way to keeping the lights on and the doors open. Losing the account wouldn't simply be a disaster for me as the VP/Account Director; it would also be a disaster for the entire global agency. Failure wasn't an option.

The solution to the difficult situation was relentless reliance on the GR Factor. The personnel at the automaker weren't especially abusive, but they were very demanding and, like so many people, quite willing to forgive themselves for their mistakes but quite unwilling to forgive others. Over-burdened with tasks, they tossed the worst of them to the agency, all the while threatening the agency with big budget cutbacks or even termination for any mistakes. They didn't plan much, and the plans they did make they frequently changed at the last second…because they could.

My staff and I could've gotten angry with them virtually every day. In the middle of a torrential rainstorm that caused some of us to be late for an 8:00 am staff meeting one key client actually threatened to lock us out of the building if we were late to any future meeting. Little slights and disrespect came almost every day. They were very clear that they were the client, and we were just the agency. We thought it was odd, since several of them on the client side had previously been employed by the agency.

We on the agency side worked in another building across town, so it was both possible and, at times, tempting to develop a culture of passive-aggressiveness and repressed anger. But I resisted that with all my strength, because I knew it would be destructive. Instead, I modeled the behavior of treating every one of them the way I would want to be treated. Partly because of that, and because I didn't initiate or allow griping-about-the-client sessions, the entire agency staff went about its business relying on the GR Factor and acting it out in client service.

Over the course of years it had two important effects. First, by refusing to cave in to resentment, by continuing to provide the very best client service our talented team could muster, we retained the account, developed many long-lasting (to this day) client relationships and did great work that kept the client's products high on the list of the media's favorites. (Great products were critical to that effort, by the way.)

The other important effect was not on the client but on each of us. While we never converted some of the command-and-control members of the client team to GR Factor followers, we were able to maintain good working relationships with them. We never had a heated disagreement, and, most importantly, we maintained our self-respect. If we had responded in kind to the small but irritating slights and disregard we faced, we would have lowered ourselves. By not trying to punch back, by not stooping to back-biting that would have brought us down, we were able to look at ourselves in the mirror each day and be proud.

To get past the destructive circle of distrust, vendors should imbue their organizations with the philosophy of treating the customer company as a true business partner worthy of respect, fairness and empathy. By making their business your business, you can succeed in what can be a very difficult area of commerce.

Chapter Nineteen

The GR Factor as Customer

Up to this point, a great deal of what you have read has discussed how to employ the GR Factor to entice, serve and retain customers. The message is a simple but powerful one. Treat others as you would want to be treated, and you will win their friendship, their admiration and their *business*. If you keep treating them that way, they will come back. And they will tell others about the great experiences you have given them. Word of mouth is the best advertising, and employing the GR Factor is the best way to build word of mouth.

At this point you might be convinced that the GR Factor can be a powerful tool. Perhaps you are already putting it to work in your business and personal relationships. Maybe you're even acknowledging strangers you see on the street or while walking the dog. Still you might ask: so what is a customer's role in all of this? Is it take, take, take and never give? Reap, but never sow? It might seem like that at times, but it shouldn't be. Not at all. The customer should not just be on the receiving end of a constant conga-line of service, warmth and approbation. A customer should be treated like a queen or king, but a customer should not act like a queen or king. The best thing to be said about monarchy is it pleases the tourists.

Very often those of us who serve customers also are customers. And when we are in the customer role it will become almost second-nature to apply the GR Factor. In the first place, if one really lives the GR Factor it is impossible to turn it off when you become a customer. And, of course, why should you? If you make every encounter a chance to treat others well, it will return enormous benefits.

Whenever I'm boarding a plane, I make certain I greet the ground attendant who is checking tickets as I approach the jetway. It amazes me how few of my fellow passengers exhibit this simple, tiny courtesy, but I can tell you that those harried people who help get us on planes safely and in a timely way appreciate it. The same holds true for restaurant servers who seem genuinely surprised – and pleased – when I ask them how they are doing after they introduce themselves at the table.

Extending this slight effort to greet others doesn't make one a saint. But given the current climate, it does differentiate you from the vast majority, who appear to find saying a kind hello to be too taxing.

Everybody likes to be acknowledged, and those who often go unacknowledged appear to like it the most. My guess is if you try this, you will find the service you get will be better than before. But getting better service is not the most important reason to extend the effort. The most important reason is the feeling you get and who you become by treating others well, by taking the high road.

When you get right down to it, there isn't much that separates us human beings from other mammals. All mammals, including humans, sleep, take nourishment and occasionally mate. But there is a trait that we humans can exhibit that most animals don't — empathy. It is an important trait, because it is a key way humans differ from animals.

I'll never forget the time I was in Mexico competing in the Carrera Pan Americana, a road race that ran from the most southern reaches of the country to the U.S. border in Texas. After one leg of the race, we were standing around taking a break in a rural corner of central Mexico when we noticed a small drift of young pigs. There were about six of them, and the way they were frolicking together was incredibly cute, almost cartoon-like. They reminded me of children in recess from kindergarten. But then a tragedy happened. A car roared up, and the driver didn't notice the piglets until the last second. Sadly, the car struck one of the pigs, killing it instantly.

It was a poignant scene, but what came next is what I'll never forget. Were the piglets saddened by the sudden death of their brother? Were they crushed by the unfortunate fate that had robbed them of their playful sibling? Did they nuzzle their wounded comrade lovingly, trying to nudge him back to life? No, all the piglets ran over to where their fallen playmate lay...*and they started eating him.*

Perhaps the social Darwinists in our midst would applaud that kind of behavior. The pig is dead, so why not make the best of the situation? You are not going to bring him back to life, *so why not eat him?*

The truth is many people in this world take the same stance with their fellow humans as the little piglets eating their recently deceased brother. Perhaps they don't do it literally, but truth be told they don't care about unfortunate circumstances that happen to others. In fact, they don't care about others at all.

I'm not saying that potential serial killers lurk on every block. I'm not saying that "psychopath" is the best way to describe your new co-worker. But I am saying that too many people refuse, reject or are simply too lazy to exhibit the distinctly human trait of empathy. Just so we're on the same page, here is *Psychology Today's* definition: "Empathy is the experience of understanding another person's thoughts, feelings, and condition from their point of view, rather than from your own."

Treating others as you would like to be treated requires you exhibit empathy. You put yourself in the shoes of others and behave as you believe they would like you to behave. It isn't just a good customer-relations technique; it actually elevates you from animal to the best example of true *human* being.

So there is far more to applying the GR Factor as a customer than just getting a smile from the waiter or a second cup of coffee when you request it. If you treat people like your equal instead of like servants, if you give each person the respect they deserve, it makes the interaction better all around. You don't simply elevate others; you elevate yourself.

The same holds true if you are a representative of a company that is a customer of another company. In that situation you might well have the power to make that a top-down type of interaction. You as the client-customer could be in the position to make life difficult, maybe even miserable, for those in the supplier company. As customer, you are the boss, and you can leverage than in all kinds of ways.

But you shouldn't.

And you shouldn't not only for everyone else's sake, but for your own sake as well.

You have probably heard the story of the harassed waiter who takes a meal from a disgruntled and abusive patron back to the kitchen, spits on it and then returns it to the obnoxious diner. Well, not only does that happen literally, it also happens figuratively.

Abusive customers virtually invite retaliation. Often that retaliation won't be blatant or obvious, but it will be very real.

The message, however, is NOT don't behave badly as a customer because someone at a store, restaurant or a vendor company will somehow make you pay. The message is to live the

GR Factor in all your dealings with others because of the good things it will bring to them and to you.

As a customer you can live in a constant state of fear and loathing. Am I getting a good deal? Am I being taken advantage of? Are these people laughing at me? And I tell you, you don't have to live there.

If you treat others as you'd like to be treated, the fog lifts, the sun comes out and life becomes much better.

Chapter Twenty

The GR Factor as an Individual

The GR Factor way of living, this way of behaving among others, has a remarkably beneficial effect in business *because it imbues business relationships with the behavior we desire and seek out in non-business situations*. When you consider the businesses that have won your loyalty and continued patronage, what characteristics do they share? Trustworthiness? Honesty? Warmth? Sincerity? And aren't these the same characteristics that you value in your friends?

The GR Factor is powerful in creating and keeping customers because it is powerful in creating and keeping relationships. Rather than making each interaction "transactional" — in other words, you do this and thus I do that — it helps makes each interaction personal. It naturally injects humanity and the important human trait of empathy into each interaction.

Just to be clear, the suggestion is not to romance each person you meet, to try to entice them or even seduce them into liking you. That would be false. At its worst that would be sociopathic. The telltale sign that it is not the desired behavior implied by the GR Factor is that you would not want to be treated that way. You don't want to be insincerely schmoozed, boozed and ultimately used. In fact you want quite the opposite of that. You want to be respected and liked by others who are sincere and truthful in their admiration for you. We call those people by a simple word — "friends."

So should you make friends with every customer, co-worker, supplier, vendor and boss? It seems like a very tall order, doesn't it? You have an affinity for some people and for others you don't. I get that. But you know what? It wouldn't hurt to try.

One thing I have observed quite plainly in my decades in the business world is that "people want to work with people they want to work with." This seemingly obvious (or perhaps even redundant) statement actually delivers a great deal of largely unspoken truth. If you are a person who treats others as they want to be treated, if you live the GR Factor minute-to-minute day-by-day, you will be a prime candidate when people you know think about hiring.

It seems that even as Human Resources recruiting functions are becoming more and more automated, personal recommendations and referrals are increasingly important in the hiring process. One big reason is this: machines can't gauge empathy. Algorithms can't determine if you'll be a productive co-worker or a malignant plague. But people can.

If you treat others as you'd like to be treated, you will have a degree of comfort when asking for a recommendation. The comfort level will exist because you'll know that your behavior has always been honorable. You have nothing to be ashamed of. You have no skeletons in your closet. You know in your heart that you would enjoy working with people who are just like you.

In contrast, picture in your mind the me-first/you-last

command-and-control boss or the selfish, back-stabbing co-worker. Do you want to work with people like that? Would you offer a recommendation or a referral to people like that?

The simple fact is this: If you are a jerk, damn few others will want to hire you, and those who do are probably jerks themselves. If you are especially calculating, you might figure you can assemble your own personal network of self-promoting organization climbers who try to get to the top by clambering on the backs of employees, co-workers and other managers. But one thing you can be certain of is that everyone in your Game of Thrones-style network is far more concerned about their own well-being than they are about yours. If they see an advantage to them in throwing you off the cliff...well, you better have your parachute on.

The way I see it you have a choice, and the choice is very clear. Do you want to put yourself in a situation in which you constantly have to watch your back to make certain one of your "friends" doesn't put a knife in it? Do you want to live and work in Jerkland? Do you want to pin your hopes and dreams of personal success on liars, cheaters and weasels whose only interest in you is how they can use you? Or do you want to live and work among caring human beings? It is really up to you.

Let me be clear about this, too, while living the GR Factor will make you a much more "hirable" individual, while in today's parlance, it will enhance your personal brand, that isn't the only reason to make the GR Factor central in the way you live your life. It isn't even the best reason. The overriding reason to live the GR Factor in all aspects of your life is the fact that it is the best way to enhance your true humanity. If only humans can truly exhibit empathy and sympathy, then individuals who treat others as they would like to be treated demonstrate those positive human traits to their fullest.

You probably see yourself as a good person. I know I do, and I know I'm not that different from you. But as I walked my dog, Austin, this morning I said to myself, "Am I really as good a person as I think I am?"

And the answer wasn't clear.

Here's why. Each person's perception of herself or himself is innately skewed, and most often that perception is skewed in his or her favor. Psychological experiments have demonstrated this over and over. The average person thinks of herself or himself as clearly above average. Psychologists call this "illusory superiority" or, more colorfully the "Lake Wobegon Effect," so named after radio host Garrison Keillor's fictional village where "all the women are strong, all the men are good looking, and all the children are above average." Sadly, it seems that Keillor might have succumbed to the syndrome himself.

If that's true, it is hard to blame Keillor, because it is a trait the vast majority of us share. As I said, illusory superior has been observed in study after study. In a seminal 1977 exploration of the topic, 94 percent of professors rated themselves above average relative to their fellow professors. Psychologists Hoorens and Buunk found that the vast majority of high school students rated themselves as significantly above-average in positive traits and significantly lower than average in negative ones. A recent survey found that more than 90 percent of drivers felt their driving skills were "better-than-average."

Citing from the abstract of a study authored by Joyce Ehrlinger, Kerri Johnson, Matthew Banner, David Dunning, and Justin Kruger, researchers found that "People are typically overly optimistic when evaluating the quality of their performance on social and intellectual tasks. In particular, poor performers grossly overestimate their performances because their incompetence deprives them of the skills needed to recognize their deficits. Five studies demonstrated that poor performers lack insight into their shortcomings even in real world settings and when given incentives to be accurate. An additional meta-analysis showed that it was lack of insight into their own errors (and not mistaken assessments of their peers) that led to overly optimistic estimates among poor performers." *

Why does this occur? Some psychologists call it a defense mechanism. They say that adopting an optimistic view of oneself can help you better cope with life's stresses. It also appears that underachievers in virtually every area can't grasp they are underachievers because, to paraphrase the landmark study alluded to above, they aren't competent enough to realize how incompetent they are. I call this "delusions of adequacy," and people who harbor those delusions are everywhere, including the management ranks of corporations, government and non-profits.

When it comes to their own goodness and their own generosity, people can hold those same delusions. They can have the sense that in terms of treating others the way they would like to be treated they are "definitely above average." But I challenge you not simply to ask the question but, more importantly, attempt to arrive at a genuine answer, not a self-reinforcing delusion.

The fact is that even the saintlike among us could probably do more to center the GR Factor in their lives. If each of us is to gain the benefits of living the GR Factor day-to-day we must be constantly on our guard that we are actually treating others as we would want to be treated rather than simply believing we are acting that way.

* *Why the Unskilled Are Unaware: Further Explorations of (Absent) Self-Insight Among the Incompetent; Joyce Ehrlinger,1 Kerri Johnson, Matthew Banner, David Dunning, and Justin Kruger*

Chapter Twenty-One

The GR Factor as a Family Member

It frequently amazes me that individuals who treat others well in everyday social and business situations can be terribly abusive, uncaring and downright mean to their family members. And they don't consider or appreciate the obvious disconnect.

You might wonder why this is being examined in a book that is about unleashing the positive aspects of the GR Factor *in business*. The answer is that to achieve all that the GR Factor can offer, it is important — as has been said many times now — that you don't simply give lip service to it or fake it but, instead, that you live it. And it is impossible to live the GR Factor if you don't practice it in your own home.

Earlier, I cited the old saying "familiarity breeds contempt." It appears that Richard Baxter in a *Christian Directory* published in 1673 was the first to deliver this message in print, but so many have done so since that the simple sentence has become a proverb. Sadly, there seems to be a great deal of truth in the saying. Just as we overestimate our goodness, intelligence and other abilities, we tend to underestimate the care we should take with our family relationships. We often let the petty annoyances of living with others unnecessarily color our relationships with them. While we are careful about the way we speak to others, we often give ourselves tacit permission to say whatever we want and do whatever we want in our own homes. And this can be hurtful and destructive.

In the extreme, a study of crime indicates that if someone is murdered and the police don't know who did it, they typically take a long look at the members of the victim's family. Family members are the prime suspects because, so often, it turns out that one of them committed the crime. And that's not hard to understand. People we live with can and often do "push our buttons" and engender disappointment, hurt and even rage. Our families bring us great joy, but they can also push some of us to the edge of violence and beyond.

Happily, most of us will never have to deal with murder, but many (most?) of us will have to deal with cruelty, self-centeredness, abuse and betrayal within our family units. Behind closed doors, many of us take off our masks of civility and find the close-knit family group gives us a license to be intolerant and abusive in ways that might amaze (and appall) our friends and co-workers. Yes, familiarity does breed contempt. But don't let your resolve to engage the GR Factor slip just because you've walked in your front door.

This is not simply a plea to avoid violence in your family. That should go without saying. This is a suggestion that you take a long look at how you treat those who are closest to you. Because they are family, are you more likely to say hurtful things to them than you would to a friend or neighbor? Are you more likely to tease them? Goad them? Or joke with them?

If you say yes to these questions, ask yourself this: how is the teasing, goading and joking being received? Does the family member on the receiving end seem genuinely to enjoy the comments? That certainly is a possibility. But there is the equal possibility that your attempts at humor are funny to you but are not at all funny to your family member.

There is also the issue of volume. Occasional teasing and jokes can be amusing and be well-received. But a continual barrage of the same kind of banter can become wearing and get old quickly. Knowing what you know about the person on the other end of your comments, do you believe your family member truly enjoys the repartee?

Further, it is not just what you say but also how you act that can make you a noxious presence in your own home. Do you contribute to the household? Do you do your fair share of tasks around the house? Are you sloppy? Are you painstakingly — and thus painfully — neat? Are your personal habits irritating, obnoxious or gross? How's your general attitude? Friendly, warm and welcoming? Or prickly and forbidding?

Of course, there is a quick test: ask yourself are you treating your family members the way you would prefer to be treated? In your home, are you behaving the way you would like your family members to behave? If the answer to both of those questions is yes, ask yourself another question: how consistent am I in treating my family members the way I would like to be treated *in every situation*?

The members of your family deserve to be the prime recipients or your empathy, your sympathy, your respect and your love. Don't let your familiarity with your family members give you the mistaken confidence that anything you say to them will be received as if it is coming from a good place. You might sincerely believe that what you say to them does come from that "good place." But what they hear might not be anything like what you believe you are saying.

It is difficult — some would say impossible — for human beings always to put others ahead of themselves. Certainly, every day we run into people of all walks of life who don't even try. But despite the fact there are instances when it might seem your life would be easier if you didn't treat others as you want to be treated, if you indulged yourself in a little bit (or a lot) of selfishness on occasion, that is not the path to a happy, fulfilling family life...and a happy, fulfilling business life.

Genuine caring can't be turned on and off. Yes, you can feign your concern for others; you can pretend to be a good person in order to get what you want and be seen as a respectable, honorable person. But over time two things will happen — others will discover that you are a fake and, more importantly, you will realize that you are a fake.

Now sociopaths never lose their self-respect, because self-respect or more precisely self-adulation is the center of their beings. But I'm inclined to believe that if you have read this deeply into the book, you are not a sociopath. Instead, you are probably like most of us, a generally well-intentioned person who values others, values family and wants to do the right thing. You will gain and enhance the respect you have for yourself by consistently — relentlessly — applying the GR Factor in your family life.

My plea is for you to adopt treating others – including your family members – no, especially your family members – in the manner you would like to be treated. With respect, empathy, generosity, trust, fairness and, perhaps most of all love and mercy.

"He who troubles his own house will inherit the wind, And the fool will be servant to the wise of heart." (Proverbs 11:29)

Chapter Twenty-Two

Can it All Be This Easy?

At this point you could well be asking yourself, "Is it that easy? Do I just treat people the way I'd like to be treated, and all will be well in my personal universe?" From long experience, I can tell you, no, it is not that easy. Enlisting the GR Factor will result in enormous benefits. You will be more successful in your business endeavors, you will gain and keep customers and your relationships with others in your business and personal lives will improve. But living the GR Factor is not always easy. And it is not that easy for reasons you might not expect.

Certainly, it is difficult to behave in a manner that is never-endingly kind, fair, respectful and empathetic. It takes effort and it takes constant self-assessment, neither of which comes naturally to us. Cognitive experts have recently theorized our way of thinking — and thus our way of acting — is inherently lazy. So to treat others in the Golden Rule manner requires us to push out of our comfort zone. What you will discover if you make that effort, however, is that it becomes easier the more you do it. If you exercise your kindness and courtesy muscles, they will get stronger. Further, the positive feedback you receive from behaving that way will motivate you to continue on that path.

So while embarking on a course that involves living the GR Factor each and every minute of each and every day is difficult and daunting, it very quickly becomes easier and easier. But what will constantly surprise you is the antagonism your behavior and demeanor can prompt in others. For reasons that are difficult to fathom, as you treat others in the manner you would like to be treated, some will simply not get it; some will insist you are "being fake," and others will actively try to sabotage you.

While you can identify several motives of people who try to block your Golden Rule path, my experience suggests that the most important of them is that your manner of living threatens their manner of living and conflicts with their world view. Those millions (billions?) who hold the belief that if you as an individual win then others must lose have a great deal of difficulty accepting a way of life that accentuates win-win outcomes. Further, those who deny the GR Factor often become jealous of the relationships you as an adherent have with your spouse, your family and, in business, your employees, your co-workers, your suppliers and, of course, your customers. Threatened as they are by the magnetic response to treating people well as a way of life, they will try to degrade your successes, ignore your advice and put obstacles in your way.

Over the decades of my career in the publishing and public relations businesses I have seen this behavior over and over. While it astounded me at first, over time I began to understand that some people — perhaps most people — generally act in a self-serving way and thus they have difficulty understanding people who don't behave that way. They consider them weak, naive or stupid and often feel free to express those opinions openly. When I think about it, they remind me of the piglets who immediately ran to eat their dead brother. In many ways they are animals who walk on two feet rather than four with instincts and inclinations no better than wild beasts. But they are out there in vast numbers, and they are threatened by the GR Factor. It doesn't register with them.

Some people who don't subscribe to the GR Factor, simply ignore those who do or accept the goodness that comes their way but fail to respond in kind. They don't reinforce your efforts to treat others the way you would want to be treated, but they don't actively put obstacles in your way either.

Then there are those who actively wage war against those who treat others as they want to be treated. Quite often these are "top-down" managers who are accustomed to using their rank in the company to command obedience. In non-business situations they couldn't lead an audience out of a burning theater, but within the halls of the business they believe a job title is all they need to lead. They are firm believers in the motto "rank has its privileges." Those of us who live the GR Factor, on the other hand, believe that rank has far more responsibilities than privileges.

There are many reasons managers adopt a top-down, I-outrank-you style. Some do it because they simply don't know any better. Often these managers come from the ranks of "individual-contributor" employees who are promoted to a supervisory role because of their performance. Their on-the-job actions separate them from their peers and deserve acknowledgement, but placing them in a managerial position with no training or mentoring puts them in a very difficult position. And with no direction to guide them in the very delicate task of managing people many respond by "acting like a boss."

Now I ask you this, how do you respond to people around you who "act like a boss?" Do you enjoy it? Do you respond positively to it? Or do you chafe at it and either openly or clandestinely attempt to work against them?

Others take a top-down approach because they feel they've put in their dues and now they should be able to enjoy the fruits of their labors. And a juicy fruit to many who have labored in the fields as a single contributor for long periods of time is to "boss other people around."

About these managers, I would ask the same questions as above. How do you respond to people who "boss you around?" Taking a step back to when you were a single contributor, were you positively motivated by people who bossed you around?

Another motivator for taking a top-down approach to management — and perhaps the most prevalent motivator — is peer pressure. Many organizations have several middle managers who are of essentially equal rank, and many of them feel they are in competition with the others to rise to the top of the managerial ladder.

One way many try to differentiate themselves from the middle-management herd is by being aggressive in the way they talk, act and manage. They believe that being a leader involves being brash, intolerant of others' ideas and self-assured to the point of arrogance. These are people who believe they can win by intimidation. They don't try to prevail based on the strength of their ideas, the quality of their work or the accomplishments of their team. They try to prevail based on sheer self-importance.

There is a subset of these top-down managers — probably a substantially sized subset — who not only attempt to manage through arrogance, but who also use arrogance to hide their basic insecurity. Subconsciously they realize that they are out of their element, that they really don't have what it takes to succeed in terms of intellectual or leadership powers, so they simply try to bull their way through. The difficulty you will run into as a GR Factor manager is that many high-ranking executives are just these kind of people. To them being brash, arrogant and abusive is a badge of strength, not a failing of character.

Managers like this are the most difficult for you as a GR Factor follower to deal with, because they are very likely to be openly antagonistic toward your management style. Since they believe in victory by intimidation, since they believe that if another wins they necessarily lose, they can't stand those who don't accept that worldview. And they are frightened to death by those who seem to succeed by treating others as they would desire to be treated. The success of GR Factor managers turns their world upside down.

In the next chapter I'll describe what it is like to live and work in an organization dominated by me-first, command-and-control managers. It isn't pretty, but it does give you a strong taste of what real world middle managers face.

Chapter Twenty-Three

Life Among the Piglets: A Real-Life Fable

I once worked for a very well known company that was, at the same time, a reasonably small family business. The brand name had national recognition, but the organization was in many ways "homely" in the best sense of that term. Co-workers treated other co-workers with respect and dignity even when they disagreed with them. Of course, there were disagreements, and passions sometimes ran high. But if there was any cutthroat, backstabbing behavior in the organization it only existed in the "leadership team" of vice presidents and in the board of directors. Even there, the organization made a conscious effort to encourage respectful disagreement versus "attacking the wounded antelope." Though the company was growing rapidly, it retained the feel of a family business operated by a benevolent patriarch. One of the company's expressed values was "humor," and that tells you

127

something right there. Not many companies explicitly value humor.

Over time the company became a more stressful place to work, and there were several reasons for that. One of the "stressors" for the company was the fact that a few years after I joined it put itself up for sale. The small investor group that owned it, prompted by an expected change in tax law, decided it was time to cash out. So naturally, just as you'd spruce your house up if you were going to sell it, the company made a very concerted effort to put its best foot forward to potential suitors. Short-term rather than long-term thinking became the order of the day. Because of this, some decisions were made that otherwise would probably not have been made, and in an effort to demonstrate additional potential the company's reach began to exceed its grasp.

Still the company was solidly profitable with an "up-and-to-the-right" sales curve. It not only survived the Great Recession, it prospered in it. All the while it retained its family-business values, and employees up and down the organization believed it was "a great place to work."

Enticed by both the value of its nationally known brand and its profitability, a number of companies stepped up as potential buyers when the business went up for sale. Some were mammoth multi-nationals; some were investment firms; some were competitors; and two were companies with which the organization had done business before. Of the two, one was considered a good partner that behaved ethically and kept its word. The other was considered untrustworthy, grasping and difficult to deal with. Sadly, when all the bids were made and the due diligence was completed, it was the offer of that last bidder — the one many regarded as untrustworthy — that the company's owners decided to accept.

One couldn't blame the owners. The bid was high — maybe higher than the company was worth — so the terms were more than acceptable. And, of course, the owners of the family-run company would never have to deal with the acquiring company again after the acquisition was completed. All they had to do was make certain the check cleared and their resort clothes were ironed.

So the little family company with the big brand name was acquired by a much larger company whose corporate culture didn't include — or even made a provision for — the GR Factor. It was a organization filled with piglets ready to eat their fallen brothers. In fact, it was a company in which the piglets often felt compelled to push their brothers in front of careening cars so they could immediately start munching on their still-warm bodies.

Of course, many of us in the acquired company's management team, myself included, didn't grasp that right away. For a long time after the acquisition some of us were able to maintain the traditions of the previous, smaller company within our departments. As the head of the editorial group, I continued to use the GR Factor as the department's north star principle. From my first days there I had hired people who shared the same values, and the assemblage continued to be a highly productive and highly creative part of what was now a much more massive and lumbering business.

But all around us the forces of me-first were gaining ground. And they were gaining ground because that's what the organization favored. This was not a company that believed in win-wins. This was not a company that believed in synergistic and symbiotic cooperation with partners, vendors and customers. This was a company that wanted to win...at any cost. It didn't care who it hurt in the process, because it really had no concern for anything but the overriding, all-important drive for bigger and bigger profits.

Now, please indulge me in a little aside here on profits. You might assume that a proponent of the GR Factor must be anti-profit or, at the very least, must believe in limiting profits. The word "profit" has been so demonized in our current society that it is natural to assume that a person who believes in treating others as she or he wants to be treated would consider profit evil. But that is just not true.

Nobody is more in favor of profits and the profit motive than I am. The quest for profits has enabled unprecedented economic growth and, more important, personal well-being. The world is a much better, kinder, more livable place because of profit. The only limits that should be placed on profits are the limits driven by the free market for goods and services. In a free market individuals vote with their dollars for the companies that provide them the goods and services that they most like. And GR Factor companies and individuals — companies and individuals who put others (customers) first — are the companies and individuals people most like. Justly earned profits are good.

But that is where the company that acquired the smaller, family business where I worked — and all companies like it — make the giant and extremely costly mistake. They believe they can attain and maintain success even as they exploit their employees, vendors, partners and customers. In almost sociopathic fashion, they believe that building profits is all they need to be concerned about, and that the relationships they have with others is secondary and unimportant. The lesson of centuries of business is: it doesn't work that way. Employees, vendors, partners and customers will not allow themselves to be exploited and abused for very long. There are other choices of places to work, clients to serve, partners to work with and outlets to buy from.

So the me-first piglet companies of the world, and the managers who run them, will eventually discover that their headlong efforts to win by making others lose is actually a losing strategy. Creative employees, stifled by the top-down management style and smothered by the exploitive atmosphere, will find other places to work. Managers who attained their positions by backstabbing will be confronted with responsibilities they can't fulfill, because they have based their career paths on politics, not achievement. Vendors who are used and abused will turn their attentions to other clients where their efforts are better appreciated and better compensated. And customers, grasping that the company is more interested in itself than in their well-being, will find other places to obtain the same goods and services, places where they feel valued.

But these are lessons that top-down, me-first management often fail to learn. Why? The experience, real as it is, doesn't match their world view. They believe for them to win, they must actively make others lose. This includes their vendors and suppliers, their employees and even their customers. It is impossible for them to grasp that other individuals won't passively allow themselves to be exploited and mistreated. They consider others sheep to be shorn.

But people are NOT sheep to be shorn. Some individuals might allow themselves to be exploited for short periods of time. But they quickly learn that there are better ways. As customers they shop elsewhere. As vendors and suppliers they serve elsewhere. And as employees they find more satisfying places to work.

Top-down, me-first managers, however, rarely learn this lesson. Their answer to sales downturns, to failed products, to heavy employee turnover is to push harder, tighten the screws tighter and take more from suppliers, vendors and employees. Since the way to promotion in those organizations is not by providing excellent customer service, innovative products and satisfying relationships, they are unprepared to compete with companies that offer those critical deliverables.

That is why top-down, command-and-control businesses fail. Innovation and excellent customer service are the keys to success in business — now more than ever — and me-first businesses don't do either well. With their exploitive, non-merit-based personnel policies they literally drive innovators from their organization. The best-and-brightest don't want nor need to work in stifling, my-way-or-the-highway organizations.

Further top-down organizations don't do a good job of

customer service, because they don't believe they have to. They see their customers as a constant stream who will always come to them. But that is a false premise because customers don't have to come to you, and they won't come to you if they find better alternatives elsewhere. Since exploitive organizations don't value their customers or their employees, they have made the job of customer service virtually impossible for themselves.

So there is a significant lesson in my experience. As much as managers like me suffered in the command-and-control environment, as difficult as it became to work day-to-day among the piglets, it was the organization that clung to its mistaken notions of how to behave that was a biggest loser.

My advice for individuals is this: If you find yourself in an exploitive company either because you didn't know what you were getting into when you were hired or because the company has been acquired by another organization with vastly different values, don't try to "stick it out." Though there are instances where companies changed their stripes and became benevolent employers who highly value customer service, in most instances expecting that change is a pipe dream.

If you live the GR Factor, you will eventually find it impossible to function in an organization that has no respect for that point of view and that management style. You might be able to survive and even thrive for a period of time, but at some point the organization's vastly different worldview will clash with yours. You can try to change the organization, but you typically will find yourself with no management support. In fact, management might be antithetical to the change you are trying to bring, even though it is in the best interest of the company. Because management's worldview differs from yours, that is a battle that will be almost impossible to win.

The alternative is to go elsewhere. Many companies are now embracing organizational policies that foster and value the GR Factor. This is sensible, because treating others as you would like to be treated is a winning business formula. It is the key to achieving great customer service, and it fosters the creation of innovative products that answer customers' needs.

Beyond those companies that actively embrace the GR Factor, there are those that are neutral on the subject. They don't actively propound treating others as one would like to be treated, but nothing about their mission, values or company policies make acting and managing in that style difficult. Because the GR Factor will bring good results, these companies will at the very least embrace the results if not officially incorporating the GR Factor into their corporate culture. These are companies in which a GR-oriented manager can thrive, because the management style will bring valued outcomes. Customers will be served better. Vendors will fulfill their obligations better. Employees will collaborate and innovate better.

On the other hand, attempting to tough it out in an organization that has no respect for others, including its own employees, is a no-win proposition. Getting that leopard to change its spots is a one-in-a-million proposition. If you stoop to fight Golden Rule detractors in the way they will understand, you run the risk of being just like them. And there is both no future and no victory in that. It is far better to find new circumstances in which living the GR Factor is valued both for what it is and for what it brings.

Chapter Twenty-Four

What Success Is

Achieving success by employing the magnetic power of the GR Factor is not just a theoretical notion but a reliable formula. Further, success achieved by adhering to the tenets suggested by the Golden Rule transcend religion, philosophy and national boundaries to extend across the business world. Treating others the way we would like to be treated is not simply the province of "religious companies," but instead presents a way of doing business – and living life – that has a proven record of success.

The United States is home to many of the world's most successful businesses, and there is a reason for that. American companies are successful because they have been created and have grown in a culture that expects and honors trust, that follows the rules of law and of ethics and that respects the rights and responsibilities of the individual. While some decry our current business climate, through the decades it was leavened with morals. These cultural norms have God's blessing.

Because of our culture, America has been a warm Petrie dish for propagating thriving businesses. In other countries that lack these cultural norms, the business of conducting business is exponentially more difficult. That is why countries that do not share our values most often find economic progress and personal growth harder to achieve. You don't have to look far across our borders to see countries whose business climate is stifling. In those countries upward mobility is a very difficult task. That is the reason that the United States has always attracted and continues to attract immigrants. The vast majority of immigrants are seeking better lives for themselves and their families — better lives that are made possible by the fact that our culture rewards those who serve others. If you offer a great product or service, customers will quite literally "beat a path to your door." And while we are dealing in cliches, America truly is "The Land of Opportunity."

Those people who think successful businesses are driven by greed are mistaken. Greed will certainly motivate you to achieve profits, but greed will also lead you astray in the very important areas of value and customer service. Greed will influence businesses to charge too much for their products and to skimp on customer service. Neither inclination will help that business succeed in the long run. In fact, either could cause the business to fail in the short run.

Contrary to what some academics would tell you, successful businesses are not driven by greed, but are fueled by two very elemental human desires. One is the innate desire of each of us to better our own situation. We strive so we may have. We get up in the morning and go to work not because we love our jobs so much, but because we like eating, having clothes on our backs and a roof over our heads. Happily, most of us in the United States are living well beyond the subsistence level. So our jobs also enable us to own vehicles, travel on vacation to a variety of places and send our children to expensive schools.

The other human desire is less obvious, but an equally powerful motivator. It is the desire to be respected and accepted both by others and, importantly, by ourselves. Gaining the respect of others is typically achieved by accomplishments – doing a good job, raising a good family, creating a valuable product or service, helping somebody. What is often overlooked is the fact that accomplishments are more important for establishing self-respect than they are for achieving the respect of others.

This begs the question: what is success?

Many people equate success with having money. The more money you have, that thinking holds, the more successful you are. Your bank statement becomes a scoreboard for your relative success or failure.

But if you look objectively at people who have a lot of money, many of them appear to be little better — or maybe a little worse — than a hot mess. They might have an impressive bank account, but they lack peace of mind. They might have an enviable assemblage of stuff — houses, cars, clothes — but they don't have enviable lives. They might capture the admiration of some, but they fail to achieve self-respect.

People can seem to have it all. But all the material goods in the world can't make up for the absence of self-worth.

Interestingly, the best way to achieve self-worth is to "give yourself away." By that I mean that you put others' well-being before your own, treating them as you would want to be treated, giving others the love, mercy and human-kindness that only our species is capable of. You might guess by behaving this way, you are opening yourself up to an endless string of abuse, pain and suffering. But in reality the opposite is the case.

Those who treat others the way they would like to be treated, those who live the GR factor every day of their lives, don't suffer for it. They profit by it. They might expend more effort than the me-first person who is constantly monitoring her or his own comfort level. They might stray out of their comfort zone into totally uncharted territory that might seem challenging and even scary. But for these small prices in discomfort they gain two very critical — and incredibly valuable things —that money can't buy: the legitimately earned admiration of others and the well-won respect of themselves.

From where I sit, having lived a long life and having known a lot of people, I am utterly convinced that your self-worth is much more important than your net worth. You can chase money, promotions, things your entire career, but in the end it is not how much money you have but how others feel about you — and how *you* feel about *you* — that really matters. It you have earned the admiration of others and yourself, you are richer than the richest billionaire on Earth.

That is what success is. It is not diamonds on fingers, cars in garages or pixels on computerized bank accounts. It is the feeling of well-being you can only attain when others love you and you love yourself.

All this means that the Golden Rule is not only a powerful prescription to achieve success in business, but it is also a powerful tool to achieve success in life.

Chapter Twenty-Five

Surviving Life's Challenges

Life beats you up. Of course, each of us has to admit compared to the generations that came before us, in many ways we have it easier. We live in an age of affluence in which most of us don't simply have the necessities; we each have a wide variety of luxuries as well. When it comes to sheer stuff, we have more of it — a lot more of it — than previous generations did. But that doesn't mean that living our lives is easy.

Life brings with it challenges, and they come in a variety of flavors: mental and physical illness, accidents, deaths of loved ones, loss of a job, failure to win a promotion, difficulties in obtaining education, drug addiction and alcoholism, child abuse, spousal abuse, betrayal, cheating. The world is filled with things that can come up to smack us in the face at any moment with no warning. There is really no way to prevent these challenges, only ways of facing them and managing their consequences. The amount of things we own and the amount of money we have can, at best, only mitigate some effects the challenges confront us, but no amount of money can help you get over the death of your Mom or the illness of your child.

We need something beyond the material to cope with difficulties. In the face of tragedy we lean on family and friends who console us with their love, understanding and nurturing. And just as we need love and mercy and healing, we should offer love and mercy and healing to others. This is the deeper message of the GR Factor. This is truly the most important aspect of treating others as you would want to be treated.

When something terrible happens — and in this life it no doubt will — you can complain about it, whine, cry foul and dwell in your victimhood. This is a perfectly natural reaction. In our world today we have come to expect that the vast majority of our days will be relatively positive and pain-free, so when disaster strikes — big or small — it is perfectly understandable to be hurt, upset and to question why such a horrible thing has happened *to you*.

The answer to that last question is as simple as it is hard to accept — the "bad thing" has happened *to you* because similar tragedies, setbacks and catastrophes *happen to all of us*. You can look at the challenge you face as a personal affront. You can whine because you feel you are being singled out. You can decry the horrible injustice of something negative standing in the way of what you believe should be a constant stream of happiness. Or you can face it head-on as an inevitable part of living.

Stuff happens. Bad stuff. Negative stuff. Stuff that knocks us right out of our comfort zone and right down to the ground. But when it happens to you it is not because you have drawn the top ticket in the Loser Lottery. It is not because you have been uniquely chosen to bear the brunt of bad times. It is because bad stuff happens to everyone. All the time.

Rather than continuing to whine about your bad fortune

— and a little whining is both understandable and therapeutic — you can try to make the best of it. Sure, wallowing in self-pity has its appeal especially in a me-oriented society where things that happen to others don't matter to you very much. But if you practice the GR Factor, you will believe that things that happen to others *do* matter to you. You wouldn't advise others to succumb to self-pity, so don't let yourself go there.

You might be saying that is much easier to write than it is to do, and I have to agree with you there. Seeing a tragedy as just another part of life is difficult when the tragedy is striking you very close to home. But at that juncture when a terrible thing has happened you have just two choices — give in to self-pity and victimhood and allow it to effect your life negatively forever or do your best to get past the negative blow as quickly as you can so you can regain an upward trajectory for your life.

When put in those terms, there is no question which fork of the road to choose. And you will find it is easier to face the challenges life puts in front of you, to face the bad stuff that comes your way, if you have the self-respect and self-awareness that comes from putting the GR Factor to work in your life.

If you treat other people the way you would like to be treated, they will respond to you. They will become your friends and they will support you, because they know that you can be trusted to do the same for them.

You might misinterpret that to mean that the suggestion is to be nice to people so they will become your friends with the endgame that you can take advantage of them. Which reminds me of the old comic's phrase, "I have so many friends that I have friends I haven't even used yet." But that is NOT what I'm suggesting. In fact, that point of view — the sociopath's point of view — is the opposite of what the GR Factor prescribes.

Using the tenet of the GR Factor you treat others the way you would want to be treated without seeking benefits or quid pro quo from doing so. What you will discover is that this method of living your life is self-rewarding. Not only will others feel better about you, but you will feel better about yourself. You will live your life with the understanding that your life has meaning to others. You will exist on a plane above the animals — the me-first piglets of the world — who care only for themselves.

The sincere regard for others without expectations of reciprocation is its own reward. Self-esteem, a sense of self-worth, peace of mind — these are the invaluable, incalculable rewards of the GR Factor.

At the same time, the sincere regard for others will win friends and supporters. When you are struck down by tragedy, they will be there to help you, to nurture you, to help you find solace.

In contrast, those who live their lives with the self-concern of the wolf in the forest will only create fair-weather friends. They will build networks of other self-serving acquaintances who use each other to climb organizational ladders or scale mountains of fame or fortune. But when hard times strike — and hard times will strike — they will find those friends vanish into their holes like mice when a cat comes on the prowl.

What the me-firsters of the world will find is that they don't have genuine friends or, at best, that the few friends they have remain their friends despite the trials and tribulations they typically put them through. Co-dependents are not the most reliable supporters in times of trouble and despair. There is the distinct possibility they might cause trouble and despair, however.

When you have people who care about you, facing difficult times will be much easier than if you don't. If your life is filled with people who like you and glad-hand you for the position you are in, not who you are, you will discover that those people will disappear the second you are not in that position. In contrast, if your life is filled with people who genuinely respect and love you for who you are, not what you are or what job you have, they will be nurturing and supportive in your times of trouble. They will come to your rescue as best they can, because they have the faith and understanding that you would do the same for them, not for any quid pro quo but because that is who you are.

That is what I mean when I say that to get the benefits of the GR Factor you have to be all in. You have to live it. You can't just fake it.

If you treat people with genuine respect and caring, those who feel and act the same way will gravitate to you. They will understand you, your efforts and how you live your life, because they are living their lives the same way. And you will discover these people — people who demonstrate their care about others but putting the needs of others before their own needs — are the perfect support group.

When you are down you are frequently in a poor position to be used as a steppingstone by others. So those who are in a relationship with you simply to use you will find spending time or even mental energy on your situation a losing proposition and will abandon you. But your friends who are like-minded about helping others and treating people well will find your worsened situation a natural outlet for their good instincts. They will get joy out of helping you back on your feet, just as you would if you were in their shoes.

Another important benefit of the GR Factor in times of difficulty is what it tells others about you. If you live your life treating others as you would like be treated, that aspect of your life will become the cornerstone of your personal reputation. Just as a company's "brand" is determined by the quality of the products it sells and the quality of the way it treats customers, so your personal "brand" — who you are to other people — is determined by the quality of your interactions with others. If you are self-concerned, self-centered and use people your personal brand will reflect that.

Your reputation is the sum-total of what people know and think about you. It is a reflection of your actions, and it has powerful effects on your future. If you treat people as they would like to be treated, you will establish a good reputation. If, on the other hand, you simply use people as stepping stones for your rise up the mountain of life, you will establish — you will earn — a bad reputation. People simply don't like being stepped on. They don't like being manipulated, messed-with and screwed around. And they will retaliate at the very least by letting others know to watch out.

I have been warned about others in my past, both in my working life and in my personal life, and I still regret the times I didn't listen to those warnings. When a friend tells you to watch out for someone, you should keep your guard up regarding that person because as nice as they might be to your face, they are likely to be equally treacherous behind your back. If an individual treats others poorly word will get out no matter how hard that person tries to disguise his or her real motives. Crowd-sourcing of information about that person will paint his or her reputation in the proper light over time.

Those who live the GR Factor don't have to worry what crowds or individuals say about them, because they have the peace of mind of knowing they treat people properly. They earn their good reputations — and all the benefits that spring from that — every minute of every day.

Treating others as you want to be treated is an excellent formula for sustainable, satisfying success in business. It will help you win customers who become your advocates. It will help you discover and retain loyal employees who enhance your business offerings. It will help you develop symbiotic relationships with your suppliers and vendors who will work with you to improve your business results.

But those effects — spectacular as they are — are simply the tip of the iceberg, the whipped cream on the sundae of what the GR Factor can bring to your life.

In the classic comedy "Harvey," the always affable but slightly muddled main character, Elwood P. Dowd, is always accompanied by his closest companion, an invisible six-foot-tall rabbit named Harvey. Asked about his philosophy Dowd replies:

"Years ago my mother used to say to me, she'd say, 'In this world, Elwood, you must be' - she always called me Elwood - 'In this world, Elwood, you must be oh so smart or oh so pleasant.' Well, for years I was smart. I recommend pleasant."

Of course, there is more to living the GR Factor than just being pleasant, but it's a start. If you treat others the way you would like to be treated, it will bring you closer to all. It will provide you with relationships that will light up your days and offer peace in the night. And it will do that because it will bring you closer to God's example of how people should live their lives.

"Love your neighbor as yourself." (Mark 12:31)

Chapter Twenty-Six

Betrayal & Healing

Life continually puts challenges in front of us. Some are more difficult to face than others. Some we triumph over easily. Others seem insurmountable. Some are the natural effects of living life — deaths of family members and friends, illness, accidents. Then there are those challenges that are brought on by others.

As a proponent of the GR Factor you will certainly have to face these challenges. One reason is that it is impossible to go through life without facing problems brought on by the actions of others. Another reason, alluded to before, is that many people who do not subscribe to the GR Factor way of life are openly antagonistic toward people who practice it. Treating others with empathy and care conflicts with their worldview that if you treat others well they are the winners and you are the loser. To use a term from the Twentieth Century, if you treat people the way you want to be treated they believe you are nothing but a "chump." What's more, many of them will try to sabotage the good you do out of jealousy, fear or resentfulness.

What do they resent? Typically, they resent the golden consequences that come to you from treating others well. Because they often behave badly and feel that is the natural course of life, they can't believe that you are behaving well out of the pure desire to act that way. They will ascribe ulterior motives to you, trying to poison the good you are bringing to the world. Many times they assume that your motives are just like theirs — self-aggrandizing and self-centered — so they believe that your selfless actions to help others are insincere and "just a front." They dearly want to believe that behind the veil of doing good for others, you are just as self-centered and self-serving as they are. They will never believe you're not.

These people are difficult to deal with, because they are rarely straightforward. Instead, they move their agenda forward by rumor, innuendo and back-stabbing. Sometimes they will be nice to your face, but they will constantly try to sully your reputation behind your back. Other times they will challenge you directly and scoff at your point of view in a manner you would never adopt simply because you believe in treating others the way you'd want to be treated. These people and the situations they bring on are difficult to deal with, but they must be dealt with. And they should be dealt with in a way that maintains the GR Factor philosophy.

Then there are the challenges brought on by others that are the result of simple human frailty. People lie; people cheat; people steal; people conspire. They give in to their darkest instincts, knowing what they do is wrong, understanding what they do can have destructive consequences, because they are not strong enough to resist temptation. Just like the little piglets eating their suddenly deceased brother, these people can't help themselves. They are not strong enough to assert their humanity in the face of temptation. Instead they bow to their animal instincts.

It is not difficult to understand why this happens. Behaving like an animal is easy. You need make no difficult decisions or moral judgments at all. You simply try to maximize your immediate situation. If there is food on the table you eat it. If there is money on the counter you take it. If there is physical gratification to be had you do it. The desires, feelings and needs of others mean nothing to you, because the health and happiness of others is subordinate to yours. Animals are the perfect sociopaths, and sociopaths are nothing but animals.

The good news is this: in a world of human beings, sociopathic behavior has consequences. And, happily, many of them are negative. Though many humans often act in the self-interested manner of animals, society has enacted laws that prohibit the most egregious forms of this behavior — murder, theft, assault and conspiracy among them. Further, societal norms mitigate against lesser offenses that are not crimes but still are expressions of animalistic behavior. But those who would do us harm to further their interests or for the sheer joy they derive in seeing others suffer are among us.

Of all the challenges we face in life, the challenges caused by others are the most difficult to deal with because it is impossible not to feel betrayed or victimized. It is impossible not to feel used. It is impossible to avoid believing that the person who did this to you should have treated you better. It is impossible not to feel bitter. We expect animalistic behavior from animals, but when humans behave like animals it is harder to accept.

Some people are weak, and they hurt us as a consequence of their weakness. Others are so thoroughly self-interested that they hurt us because they believe it will help them.

The important question is: how should we respond to these injuries and the people who cause them?

The answer is within the GR Factor itself. We should respond to these hurts and offenses by treating the offenders the way we would like to be treated. And the way we would like to be treated is with fairness, honesty and mercy.

When we are hurt by others it is all too natural to want to "get back at them." "Don't get mad; get even" is a common phrase that sums up a way to respond to pain caused by others. But if you seek revenge, you run the risk of behaving as badly as the person who hurt you. You give away the best part of your humanity in an effort to somehow get even. But getting even is a fool's game. The best way to respond to bad behavior, to greed, to thoughtlessness, to betrayal, is not by stooping to become as bad and inhuman as the offender. The best way is to succeed as a human being far beyond the place the offender could ever dream of succeeding.

How do you do this?

You do it by positively but at the same time relentlessly applying the GR Factor. Treat others the way you would want to be treated. It is not conditional. The Golden Rule does not say "treat others as they treat you."

There is a reason for that, and it is not simply blind altruism. Those who do falter in their efforts to follow the GR Factor and stoop to seeking quick revenge or retribution lose the best part of their humanity. They succumb to bitterness and anger, and, importantly, they let bitterness and anger control them, sometimes even become them.

That is the trap that the GR Factor enables you to avoid.

Bad things happen to us all. Some of these bad things are caused by bad people or by weak people who give in to badness. Do you want bad people and weak people who can't avoid temptation to be the focus of your life?

It is far better *for you* as an individual to maintain and enhance the best aspects of your humanity, the best aspects of your soul that separates you from the animals, by continuing to do your very best to treat others as you would prefer to be treated.

By doing so you can escape bitterness. You can avoid wasting your precious energy on revenge, and you can make certain that it doesn't drag you down or hold you back.

This will become your advantage. While others battle, while others play the game of tit-for-tat or if you hit me I'll hit you back, you will dwell at a level above the fray, the noise and the rancor. You will spend your energy helping others, not just for what it gives them but for what it gives you.

Succeeding is great revenge. Succeeding for the right reasons is the best revenge. Don't bow to becoming one of the problem-givers. Instead, call on your best self to become a problem-solver, and you will find it will solve your problems as much as it will help you solve the problems of others.

"Let no corrupt word proceed out of your mouth, but what is good for necessary edification, that it may impart grace to the hearers. And do not grieve the Holy Spirit of God, by whom you were sealed for the day of redemption. Let all bitterness, wrath, anger, clamor, and evil speaking be put away from you, with all malice. And be kind to one another, tenderhearted, forgiving one another, even as God in Christ forgave you." (Ephesians 4:29-32)

Chapter Twenty-Seven

Missing the Point: A True-life Parable

As you incorporate the GR Factor into your life on a daily basis, you will discover an interesting phenomenon — you become very sensitized to others' behavior. One reason for this is because you are so intent in your desire to treat people the way you want to be treated that you pay a great deal of attention to how individuals treat each other. Perhaps you are clandestinely looking for kindred spirits who think and act in the manner you do. Perhaps you are seeking better ways to serve others.

No matter the reason, this penchant to examine others' actions has an interesting effect. When you see people who don't treat others well or who don't treat you well, you might get angry about it...maybe angrier than if you weren't paying so very much attention to how people behave toward others.

This can be negative. Very negative. It could be described

as an unintended consequence of the GR Factor, and because it is potentially destructive, it needs to be acknowledged, examined and counteracted. Anger — even righteous anger — is not a good thing. It can hurt the person who is the object of the anger and, more important, it will hurt the person who is angry. Whether held inside or expressed openly, anger is always harmful to the person who experiences it.

As a true believer in the GR Factor, as a person who attempts to treat everyone the way I would want to be treated, I must admit that when I witness people who are mean, cruel and uncaring, it makes me mad. And when mean, cruel or uncaring behavior is directed at me I get angry. Typically, I don't express that anger, but I do get "righteously pissed off" sometimes. (I have to note, in candor, that my family might tell you my "righteous anger" does have a way of getting expressed occasionally, too. And I'm not proud of that.)

I'm a bit ashamed to admit that I can be prideful about the manner I behave toward others. I try to make a honest effort to do the right thing. So when people don't treat others well or don't treat me well, I have difficulty understanding why they fail to understand their behavior is not only wrong but also self-defeating. That failure to grasp what to me is obvious upsets me. But I have to admit there is more to this. When someone is intentionally deceitful, cruel or just plain mean to me, I have a great deal of difficulty understanding why that person would treat me, who always makes a sincere effort to be kind and generous, in such a callous, unfeeling manner.

Part of that is their problem, based on their behavior — but part of it, my reaction to it, is my problem, based not only on my belief in treating others with care, but also in my pride, which I shamefully admit may very well be unfounded, in how nicely I treat others.

First, the possibility (likelihood?) exists that I don't treat others nearly as well I perceive I do. Second, even if you do treat people pretty well pretty much all of the time — as I try to do —

you shouldn't be prideful about it. You should simply view what you do as behaving properly, rather like stopping at stop signs and putting the top back on the toothpaste tube. In other words, I, or anyone, who treats people well shouldn't be self-congratulatory about it.

"But you, O man of God, flee these things and pursue righteousness, godliness, faith, love, patience, gentleness." (1 Timothy 6:11)

The following story from my life illustrates that just because a person or a company says it follows the precepts of the GR Factor doesn't mean it actually conducts its business that way. You're an adult, so that should come as no surprise to you. What can come as a surprise are the internal assumptions you begin to build about others when you adopt the GR Factor as your mode of conduct. I firmly believe in the GR Factor, but it is critical to note that, in those who live their lives that way, it can set up expectations that won't be fulfilled. And in the very real world in which we all live, that can create problems that need to be acknowledged and addressed.

Here is a true-life story that illustrates that:

Several years ago when I worked in the public relations field, the global car company that was my firm's client was acquired by another global car company. The acquiring company then followed form and fired our public relations agency and hired an agency closely allied to them. It happens all the time, and though our agency had taken the acquired car brand from fifty thousand annual sales in the United States to two-hundred-and-fifty thousand in a five-year period, it wasn't unexpected. It did, however, leave me in the position of having to find a new job.

This is where living the GR Factor was a definite benefit to me. In previous years I had done a great deal of freelance speechwriting for an event management firm owned and managed by a famous television personality. The speeches for executives in various businesses had gone well, and I ended up writing speeches for the TV personality when he did motivational and business events. During the course of several of these jobs I had met and won the trust of a well-known TV producer who staged live events like vehicle introductory shows.

Just as my job was coming to a close for the public relations agency, the producer — a great guy named Dan — called me and told me he had someone he wanted me to meet. So I went to lunch with him and met a guy named William who was in the process of setting up an event-management operation for a company that was based Back East. Blessed with Dan's endorsement, I had a good meeting and hit it off with William.

He told me that the company for which he worked was founded by and filled with devoted Christians.

"Some people have trouble working in that kind of environment," he said. "They start some meetings with prayers, for example."

Well, that did seem a bit unusual to me, because none of the many companies I had worked for in my career conducted business that way. But I figured there are far worse things than expressing your religion in the workplace.

I met with the people I had to meet with, found them pleasant and industrious, and when the job was offered I listened to the manager's offer of employment closely. He told me he was looking for a person who could both edit written pieces to make them ready for new-business proposals and plan an event the company was seeking to do in a few months' time. He also mentioned he needed someone to write a general description of the services the business offered, which would also be used in soliciting new business. Apparently, he and his small staff were having some difficulty describing what they did.

That all sounded fine to me. I was confident I could complete the assigned tasks in excellent fashion, because I have both the experience and the skills necessary. At that point I had been editing for very successful magazines like *Motor Trend* and very successful websites like Kelley Blue Book for a couple of decades. I had also planned numerous events for those publications, and I had planned international media events for global car manufacturers during my lengthy stint in public relations.

At the time, I had the good fortune to know a career counselor, and he advised me, "Don't be in such a hurry to get a job that you take the wrong job." That advice was ringing in my ears as I discussed the position with the manager of the business unit. The job wasn't what I really wanted, and it didn't require the people-management skills I had acquired and refined through the years. In my mind, I questioned whether I would mesh well with the others on the staff.

And then the manager said something very telling to me. He said, "We try to treat others as we want to be treated."

Well, as you can guess, that really resonated with me. When I heard that phrase, I said to myself, "Maybe this could be the right place for me." So I accepted the position. What I did not realize was that my perception of "treating others like I want to be treated" might be very different from others' perception of it. And that's on me, not on them.

The manager then asked me to complete a writing assignment he had previously given me as a sort of test, for which I would be paid as a freelancer. I was confident that I could finish that assignment without difficulty because it involved the kind of writing I had been doing for decades. In my heart of hearts, I believed that once I turned in the writing assignment, the work would provide additional proof that adding my talents to the staff on a full-time basis was a good idea.

So I completed the assignment, sitting at my home office desk where I'm writing this, and I turned it in to my new boss. He didn't like it.

I was stunned. Typically the reaction to the assignments I turn in is "Thank you very much. When can you write something else for us?"

But my newest "boss" liked neither the content of the piece nor the way it was presented. He gave me a little lecture on what to write and how to write. Now, that is his prerogative as the manager of the business unit, and I readily acknowledge that. But I also know that I'm a pretty good writer. I've been earning my living as a writer for decades, and I know a thing or two about the craft. Maybe even a thing or three.

Needless to say, my internal reaction to the lecture wasn't all that positive. Okay, being totally honest, it was decidedly negative. I felt I had worked hard on the assignment, had provided a significant amount of useful information and had delivered it in a colorful, readable way. But the manager — my boss — didn't like it, and he has the final say.

So I checked my ego in a locker and listened closely to what he had to tell me. First, he said the piece didn't cite enough facts. Then he said he didn't like the way it was written. As mentioned, I was amazed by this because, throughout my very lengthy career as a professional writer, the predominant comments about my work have been extremely positive. Editors from a wide variety of fields have praised the clarity and quality of my writing.

I listened intently to his suggestions about how I could revise the work to bring it to the company's standards, which essentially were my boss's personal writing standards. I learned that by "facts" he sought to quote "hard numbers." Don't bother with analysis. Don't bother with context. Just ladle on "the facts."

Okay, I thought, I can add facts. Facts aren't hard to come by, especially if you don't need to explain what they mean.

Then there was the matter of the writing itself. You can judge for yourself, but I've always believed — because I've been told it many times — that my writing style is clear yet colorful. It conveys the message with a lilt of lightness or even humor. Well, lightness was not his thing.

He insisted on a writing style that is consistently dull.

He favored simple declarative sentences.

He did not like compound sentences.

He relentlessly removed adjectives and adverbs.

He wanted only the simplest verbs.

He liked one-sentence paragraphs.

As you can see from the past six paragraphs, that style of writing is not all that pleasing.

Of course, I didn't learn the preferred style right away. At first, I continued to write the way I have always written, not quite understanding his desired style — largely because I couldn't imagine how that style could be desired. But I was beaten down by the subsequent editing of material I believed was well-written.

And perhaps that was the biggest issue. It wasn't simply that the manner in which I write is different than the style this business desired. It was that my style of writing was demeaned...and I felt demeaned.

Here I was, a very successful writer-editor with several well-received books to my credit and a legacy of literally thousands of articles published in prestigious publications, and I was being treated like a somewhat slow-witted intern. What was most troubling to me was the fact that I definitely was not being treated the way I would want to be treated, not in the way that I have treated the scores of writers who have worked for me, a few of whom were slow-witted interns.

As I mentioned, another of my responsibilities was to edit the writing assignments of others. This task was burdening the manager who hired me as the volume of new-business proposals grew. In one instance, I was given an article written by a staff member to edit, and I discovered the original work very amateurish. The assignment was to write about a prospective client's vehicle, but ninety percent of the article was devoted to the discussion of loading the vehicle for a trip. Just two or three paragraphs actually dealt with other aspects of the vehicle like, importantly, the driving experience.

I thought seriously about simply sending it back to the writer, who was a crony of the manager, with the suggestion that it be re-written to be less about packing and more about the overall aspects of the vehicle. Looking back, maybe that is what I should have done.

Instead, believing there might be negative "political" consequences if I just sent it back for a re-do, I decided to approach it in the way I had approached similar situations in the past when I didn't have full editing authority. I did a heavy "line-edit," meaning I retained the basic structure but fixed the grammatical, spelling and punctuation errors, of which there were many. I cleaned up some odd sentence structures and revised some physical descriptions.

The typical response to this from most professional writers with whom I've worked is thanks. Occasionally — so few times that they are hard to remember — a writer will question a change or two I suggest but applaud the others. In the vast majority of cases, not only is there no argument, there is sincere appreciation that, together, we have made a better piece.

Not so in my first editing test at the new company. Instead, the writer was personally offended by my suggested changes. I wasn't privy to the entire discussion he had with the manager, but I did hear that he complained that I was "changing the voice" and taking all of the personality out of the piece. Well, if poor spelling, bad grammar and clumsy descriptions are "the personality," I guess I did.

After that, I was rarely given writing to edit, even as I learned the company's desired style. You know...

Start with a simple declarative sentence. Write another simple declarative sentence. Then write another.

Start a new paragraph with a declarative sentence.

Throw in a partial quote "to lend authenticity."

Okay, you get it. This is not my style. It is also not remotely standard publication style. In fact, it is nearly the polar opposite of good writing.

At this point, I had two choices: I could tell them that I found it impossible to write and edit as they wanted, or I could try to understand their style and write and edit to their standards. From my current perspective, perhaps I should have done the former, but I attempted to do the latter. And I think I arrived at a place where I wrote my assignments in the manner they desired. I hated to turn them in, but I did write them that way.

It wasn't enough.

I got very few editing assignments. My writing assignments were heavily revised by the staffer who had composed the first piece I was given to edit. It was a painful process to me to see writing I was proud of turned into something less than it was before.

Then there was the event I was supposed to plan and manage. As the weeks unfolded it became clearer and clearer that I wouldn't get the chance to plan the event after all. I sat in the office day after day as others — usually the manager and his buddy — did virtually all of the planning right in front of me. Though I was, by far, the most experienced member of the group in planning such an event, I was relegated to doing some of the detail and support work.

The company was a vendor supporting big, multinational clients. Often those clients were very demanding. The business unit that employed me was tasked with getting new business from new clients, sometimes an even tougher task. The workload was heavy and frenetic. It was no picnic, but that's why they call it "work." While I would have appreciated a less hectic pace, I absolutely understood it. My fellow colleagues and I, by our salaries alone, were burning the company's money, and we weren't bringing any revenue in. The pace seemed appropriate.

I did have difficulty with the randomness of overnight travel though. Several times I walked in the office in the morning and was told to go home to pack, because we were leaving for another city across the country in the afternoon. Often we'd land in the Eastern city after an overnight flight, and, with no sleep at all, immediately go into all-day meetings. Sometimes these meetings were with clients, but often they were internal "brainstorms" meant to surface ideas that would help us win clients.

Now I don't know about you, but I don't typically come up with my best ideas after being without sleep for twenty-four hours. But in this company, that was standard procedure. Was it the way I would want to be treated? Even more to the point, was it the way I would treat others?

But the thrust of this story is not that the company was very demanding of its employees, sometimes pulling them away from their families for days on end with no notice, often leaving them over-tired and uncomfortable. None of that is appealing, but I realized: many workers are over-tired and uncomfortable every day of their working lives.

Looking back with the perspective of time, the most troublesome part of my employment in this company that proclaimed it wanted to treat others the way they would want to be treated is that I did not believe I was being treated with respect. I could have come to terms with everything about the company — the demanding hours, the random travel, the differences over what represented quality work — if my bosses had expressed some admiration for my contributions to the team and some regard for my work. In other words, if I had received some good old-fashioned encouragement.

In contrast, overall I got the distinct impression that my judgment was not trusted and my experience and skills not respected. That was distinctly not the way I would have asked to be treated. That is not the way I would have treated others had I been in the position of authority. And, in a strict business context, that is not the way to motivate productive efforts that will bring good results.

But in defense of my boss, I sincerely believe the way I was treated was the way he felt comfortable being treated. Maybe it was the way he had been treated by his superiors through the years. I am certain that he was not trying to be abusive or dismissive. And I am certain that he is a good person who cares about others, including, importantly, people he employs and manages. But employing and managing people is difficult. It is stressful. It requires constant decision-making. You sincerely want to do the right thing, but in the pressure of the moment, you do the wrong thing, the expedient, less-demanding thing. I've been there many times, and I know. The bottom line here: It wasn't them; I was expecting too much. I was projecting my standards and desires on others, and that's a path to disappointment.

So aside from revealing myself as a sometimes whiny underling, what is the takeaway from all this? Parables are designed to teach. What lesson does this teach?

It taught me several valuable things. First, and I believe very obviously, don't tell others one thing and then do another. Yes, things change, but as you set up expectations it is important to either fulfill them or, at worst, explain why they are not being fulfilled. Don't "talk the talk" and then fail to "walk the walk."

If you decide to make the GR Factor your North Star as a manager — and as a person — your goal should be to treat others as you would want to be treated, and, if you sense you are failing to live up to that promise, at the very least acknowledge it and, if you can, explain why. The parable I just recounted is a very clear demonstration of the importance of the admonition that you must live the GR Factor; you can't use it like a crowbar when you need it and put it in the back of your toolbox the rest of the time.

My manager in the business I described in this chapter, whom I believe to be a good and thoughtful man, just couldn't find it in himself to trust me. Perhaps he'd been burned by others in the past. (Which of us hasn't?) Perhaps he was so eager to do well that he couldn't bear to cede control of anything he deemed important...and he deemed everything important. In any case, his words set up an expectation of conduct that, as I saw it, wasn't fulfilled, and that was worse than if no expectation of conduct had been created in the first place.

In other words, if you say you are going to make the GR Factor the standard for your behavior, then MAKE THE GR

FACTOR THE STANDARD FOR YOUR BEHAVIOR. Don't pretend you care about others. Don't waver between kind, caring merciful behavior and self-serving, self-centered conduct. If you do, you'll destroy any advantages you might have gained by quoting the Golden Rule in the first place.

But beyond what my former boss might learn from this chapter in my life, there is also what I learned about myself and my own conduct. Certainly I learned that I was disappointed. I learned for the "nth" time that you can't always believe what you hear. You might say, I set myself up for disappointment by expecting more than I had reason to expect. People aren't always their best selves. You have to be aware of that and show mercy towards it. But I learned much more for the experience.

Despite my disappointment at promises that I felt were unfilled, I decided I would try to stick it out and continue to treat others, most especially my boss and co-workers in the venture, exactly as I would want to be treated. I tried to quell my inner anger and respond positively to all requests. Further, I decided that, rather than sulking, I would do all I could to make the event I thought I was hired to plan as successful as it could be, despite the fact that I hadn't planned it.

In short, I continued to live the GR Factor. And it worked wonders. For the first time at the organization, I began to feel that my contributions were being seen and appreciated. I got the impression that instead of being viewed as a marginal employee, to be tolerated, I was being seen as a valuable team member. More responsibilities were given to me, and I began to feel that my experience and opinions were starting to be valued. Not only did the business relationships get better, the personal relationships with the small new-business team became stronger, too.

Did it become my "dream job?" No, it didn't. Did I forge deep, never-ending relationships with individuals on the staff? No, I didn't. But responding to a potentially negative, disappointing situation in a positive way, rather than throwing in the towel and resorting to self-pity and anger, was transformative.

It worked. It made the situation very much better than before.

Treating other people the way you want to be treated is the right thing to do, not just for them, but for you. It helps alleviate anger, bitterness and resentment, and it helps build self-esteem and happiness. You will never be perfect at applying the GR Factor. I know I will always be far from perfect in applying it. But I also know that my sincere attempt to live and behave in that manner is the best course for me...and the best course for you. And I have assurances of that from the Highest Authority.

"The work of righteousness will be peace, And the effect of righteousness, quietness and assurance forever." (Isaiah 32:17)

Chapter Twenty-Eight

Justice & Mercy

Few of us find it natural or easy to extend forgiveness to people who have hurt us. We are not wired that way. When people feel threatened or are attacked, the natural inclination is to fight back. Your body responds automatically with a rush of adrenaline to enable you to better defend yourself. Certainly if your life is threatened or someone seeks to do bodily harm to you or others, fighting back physically is justified. You don't expect others to stand idly by as they or their loved ones are assaulted, so you cannot be condemned for confronting physical violence aimed toward you with force.

But in situations in which the affront is non-violent, a different response — guided by the GR Factor — is called for. Treat the offender as you would want to be treated if you were the offender.

And how would you like to be treated as one who has hurt another?

I believe you would like to be treated with justice and with mercy.

The responses here are complex because justice might suggest one outcome, and mercy would suggest another. For example, let's take one of the most heinous instances of hurting another, murder.

For taking another person's life, justice would suggest that proper punishment is for the offender to forfeit his or her life. Mercy, on the other hand, would suggest a milder penalty.

Happily, we don't have to confront murder and murderers in our lives very often. But we do have to deal with people who hurt us all the time. And we also have to be aware of the fact that we hurt others. Often it is inadvertent; sometimes it is the result of weakness in the face of temptation; and sometimes it is simply the result of consciously doing the wrong thing.

In those instances where we do wrong — for whatever reason — my guess is we would prefer to be treated with a larger dose of mercy and a smaller dose of justice. And that understanding should guide our behavior.

Each of us is imperfect. We make mistakes; we misunderstand situations; we behave badly. Justice suggests we be punished for those indiscretions in ways that match the offenses. But mercy implies a different course.

The GR Factor does not require you to ignore or somehow endorse bad behavior directed your way. It doesn't mean you allow yourself to become a human punching bag for others. But it does suggest that you respond to the negatives piled on you by others in a way that you would want and expect to be treated if you were the offender, not the victim.

As I said at the beginning of this chapter, that is not easy. That does not seem natural, because "natural" behavior is typically more self-centered. But this "learned behavior" is both the "right" way to act and the best way to act.

If you respond to offenses against you by understanding and accepting the injustice of the act and treating the actor with both fairness and mercy, you will be expressing the best part of your humanity. Further, you will discover that such a response frees you from anger and bitterness.

Anger and bitterness that you hold inside, that consume you, do nothing to punish the perpetrator of the bad act. You might think your anger will hurt them, but what you will find if you look deeply is that it hurts you. It ruins you day; it wastes your time; it worsens your outlook on others.

Expressing mercy and forgiveness to those who hurt us is not nearly as beneficial to those we forgive as it is to us. People who are at the core self-centered do not care for a second whether their victims forgive them or not. They have no moral compass that guides their behavior, so they don't believe that any of their actions, no matter how heinous, are wrong. Sociopaths believe that anything that gives them pleasure, gratification or advances their desires is "right." Anything that stands in the way of their pleasure or gratification is "wrong." Your forgiveness is meaningless to them.

It is meaningful to you, however. It enables you to move on. It enables you to throw off the burden of bitterness that could otherwise destroy your life. You don't want to dwell in the land of anger. It sucks the joy out of day-to-day living.

Every day we are given opportunities to show kindness, mercy and love to others. We can take those opportunities by offering a word of encouragement, saying something kind or even just acknowledging a stranger with a hello. Or we can stay in the tunnel of ourselves.

Many people choose to stay in that tunnel of themselves, and it is hard to understand why. It is dark, cold and lonely in that tunnel. The walls are dripping, and the smell is dank.

When you bring the GR Factor into your life, you emerge from that tunnel. You go from the darkness into the light. You enter the sunshine, the place where things look better, feel better, even smell better. You feel the warmth of the sun on your shoulders, and you know you are in the right place.

Don't spend another day, another hour, another minute, another second in that tunnel of yourself. Instead, come into the light of treating others as you want to be treated. And not just when it is convenient for you or when it won't put you out but every tick of every day.

Yes, it will be good for all who meet you. Yes, your help, support, kindness and love will enhance their lives. Your family will benefit. Your friends will benefit. Your co-workers will benefit. And your community will benefit.

But the biggest beneficiary of embracing and living the GR Factor is you. It will transform the way people think about you, and, more importantly, it will transform the way you think about yourself. That is the undeniable power of treating others as you would want to be treated.

Chapter Twenty-Nine

Real World Successes

Since you've read this far I am confident that you sense the value and power of The GR Factor. As you've been reading you have no doubt identified individuals and businesses that have exemplified the philosophy of treating others as you would want to be treated. In this section I will take a look at a number of businesses big and small that, in their actions, demonstrate a high regard for The GR Factor. Many of the businesses discussed here might not overtly make following the Golden Rule a business policy. In fact some might shy away from acknowledging their reliance on The GR Factor, perhaps fearing that it is too "religious."

Oddly, these days being religious is often viewed negatively, although it is hard to imagine what could be wrong with following the almost universally held tenet that it is good and proper to behave toward others the way you would like them to behave toward you. Wouldn't the world be a better place, I have to ask, if more people comported themselves that way?

In any case, the following examples examine a variety of successful businesses, large and small, showing how The GR Factor enables them to thrive by serving others.

Southwest Airlines

I am old enough to remember where an airline flight was a special and pleasant experience. On my first airline flight from Chicago's Midway Airport to Miami in the dead of winter in 1958, my dad, brother and I donned sports coats and neckties for the flight while my mom wore one of her best outfits. The pace was genteel and the service was elegant. As I remember it — and I do remember it pretty well — even the food was good. It was, of course, served on china plates with real flatware and drinking glasses made of (go figure) glass.

These days airline travel on most carriers is as removed from genteel as the WWE is removed from the Joffrey Ballet. Worse than that, though, the service, such as it is, resembles the loading and unloading of a cattle car and the demeanor of many flight attendants makes the Wicked Witch of the West seem like Mother Teresa.

Southwest Airlines is succeeding mightily against the contemporary tide of airline "customer handling" by consistently applying The GR Factor in the way its people treat customers. Its flight attendants, ground personnel, pilots and co-pilots are almost universally friendly and pleasant. They don't bark orders at their customers. Instead, they try their best to help and, amazingly, they seem to have a sense of humor. They riff on the boarding and de-planing announcements. On more than one occasion I've heard them break into song and lead the passengers in a chorus of happy birthday.

Southwest Airlines also treats its passengers as they would want to be treated by not charging them to check a suitcase or change a flight. And its fares are typically the lowest or among the lowest from point A to point B (two very popular destinations.) If you haven't heard, people like saving money.

So here is what you get on a Southwest flight — a low fare, no fee for bag check, a pleasantly helpful crew and, if you want it, a snack. To me it adds up to the pervasive use of The GR Factor.

JACK R. NERAD

Nordstrom

This has been a tough decade for brick-and-mortar retailers. Online competitors like Amazon have taken a giant bite out of department stores and speciality retailers, but Nordstrom has persevered largely because it has always made The GR Factor the guiding rule of its customer relations. In a climate rife with indifferent store clerks, poorly organized selections and dingy, seen-better-days retail environments, Nordstrom is a breath of fresh air. And at times I mean that quite literally. Walk into a Nordstrom after a foray elsewhere in Localmall USA, and you will find yourself walking into a completely different experience that literally smells better.

Not only are the physical stores attractive, well-organized and a pleasure to navigate, but they are also populated (heavily populated) with store personnel who seem very eager to help. Yes, I acknowledge that their sales clerks are compensated to do so, but so what? If it takes a well-directed compensation policy to reinforce The GR Factor, so be it.

Finally, in a response to online retailers, Nordstrom has created an elegant, upscale buying site of its own that is attractive and easy to navigate. Whether you buy online or in a Nordstrom retail store, you can be assured that your satisfaction is guaranteed. My lovely wife Sandi, a truly gifted shopper, buys and buys and buys from Nordstrom knowing that if the dress, blouse or pants aren't right when she gets them home she can return them for an exchange or refund with zero hassle. Yes, she does return some purchases to Nordstrom from time to time, but she buys much more than she returns, and I have the bills to prove it. The GR Factor? You bet.

Chick-Fil-A

Most fast-food restaurants are dreary places that seem to collect dreary individuals. The operative phrase seems to be "get in and get out as fast as you can." You order at a counter hoping against hope that the person taking your order is actually entering it properly, and then you stand around waiting for your order to come up. Furtively, you peek into the bag to see if you won the fast-food lottery and your food is as you requested it. If you decide to "eat in," you go to the indifferently cleaned table and sit in the uncomfortable chair that is designed to prevent you from lingering.

Then there is Chick-Fil-A, a truly different vibe in a fast food restaurant. As you walk in, you are often greeted by an employee who is in the midst of cleaning a table or delivering something to a customer. At the counter you are warmly greeted by the order taker, and by the way they treat you — the way you want to be treated — you not only build confidence that your order will be right but that this is a very pleasant place to buy and eat a meal.

When your order has been taken you can go right to your table, because it is Chick-Fil-A's policy to deliver the meal to you, not to subject you to hanging around the counter waiting for your order to arrive. As the meal is delivered to you, the person who delivers it asks if there is anything else they can do for you. And it seems like they really mean it. Not only that, but when you request something, they actually do it for you. When you thank them, their response is always the same, "It's my pleasure."

That is the GR Factor to the highest order. When we treat others the way we would want to be treated, and it is not a burden; it genuinely is our pleasure.

Doug Murdick's Fudge

Decades ago when I was a kid, our family would vacation in Traverse City, Michigan. That made a lot of sense since my grandmother was born there, and we had a lot of relatives in town. I have a thousand pleasant memories that involve Traverse City, but among the most pleasant are the family visits to Doug Murdick's Fudge, a small storefront fudge shop on, yes, Front Street. At Doug Murdick's Fudge you could watch the employees prepare a batch of fudge in big copper kettles and then see them pour the marvelous concoctions onto marble tables for cooling and slicing. But wonderful as that was, it was nothing compared to tasting that amazing, creamy, flavorful fudge. Chocolate fudge, maple fudge, fudge with walnuts, cherry fudge with cherries in it and my personal favorite — the sinfully rich, lusciously smooth vanilla fudge. To top it all off, you bought your slabs of fudge from helpful, personable, small-town people who knew how to say hello and thank you very much and hope to see you again.

If only there were a place like Doug Murdick's Fudge today, you might be saying to yourself. Well, there is. And it's called Doug Murdick's Fudge. It is still on Front Street, still a couple doors down from the drug store my grandfather and cousins used to own, and it still does business the same way they did it way back in 1964 when I was a kid. I know that because I visit them now and then and because I call them several times a year — yes, call with a telephone — to order fudge for my friends, family and, yes, I admit, for myself. (That vanilla fudge might be about the best thing I've ever tasted.)

Why is Doug Murdick's Fudge still around and still thriving 50+ years after opening its doors? It is because the business has remained both true to its customers and true to itself. I'm certain that through the years there must have been temptations to change the recipes, cheapen the product and skimp on the customer service. In an era that says go big or go home, Doug Murdick's Fudge has remained comfortably small so it can concentrate on making great fudge and selling it in a way that customers appreciate. Yes, you can buy their fudge online these days, but I recommend giving them a call instead. Each person I've spoken to there has been pleasant and helpful, so for the price of one phone call you can see what living in a small town in mid America in 1964 was like. I think it was pretty darn good.

Starbucks

Coffee — tasty brown water served for $3 a cup. On the face of it, the business proposition is a difficult one. Coffee is served pretty much everywhere from gas stations, to diners, to fine restaurants. So what makes Starbucks so successful? Well, there is no doubt that its coffee drinks are a variation on what we usually expect, but cappuccinos, lattes and frappes are not the exclusive province of Starbucks. So how does the company differentiate its locations from others? A large part of it is how it treats it customers and how it treats its employees.

Typically, restaurants and coffee shops don't want their customers hanging around after they've "finished." The thinking has always been to "turn the table," opening up space for new customers. But Starbucks stood that idea on its ear by listening to their customers and determining that many of them want a warm, welcoming place to spend time. Based on that idea of treating customers the way they want to be treated, Starbucks has installed easy chairs, tables that serve as desks and wi-fi to enable customers to make Starbucks a home away from home or, in many cases, an office away from the office. (One of my former direct reports used do a "Starbucks morning" two or three times a month. It was a change of scene for him that, if anything, improved his production. Of course, he had a GR Factor boss who enabled it.)

Starbucks employees also routinely learn return customers names and typical orders, often preparing their coffee creations before they even get to the cash register. While walking our dog, my wife would find that her coffee was being made even as she tied Austin up outside our local Starbucks. Yes, you might find a barista here or there with attitude, but most Starbucks team members give you a positive experience.

And Starbucks' emphasis on The GR Factor doesn't end with the way customers are treated. The company also delivers uncommonly good benefits to its in-store employees. The wages are good, and Starbucks offers its employees health care and other perks that are rare in the quick-service restaurant business. Obviously, Starbucks under the leadership of longtime (and now former) CEO Howard Schultz determined that "love thy neighbor" is the right business philosophy for the worldwide organization.

Marriott Hotels

Many of the businesses described in this section of the book make positive customer service a very high priority, but they don't explicitly cite the Golden Rule as their guiding principle. Marriott Hotels is different in that it has made the Golden Rule — and hence the GR Factor — it's North Star.

This is directly from Marriott Hotels' website:

We live by the Golden Rule.
Treating others like we'd like to be treated.
It has always been our guiding principle.

It is also the reason that Marriott Hotels — a mammoth, multi-national company that operates an impressive number of hotel chains aimed at different customers — has been so successful. Being explicit about employing the power of the GR Factor has immediate and long-term benefits to any business that lives it every day.

The Marriott Hotels' site includes a heartwarming collection of customer stories indicating quite clearly that its employees around the globe are taking the Golden Rule to heart and expressing it in their work.

Here are a few telling examples of the GR Factor at work in the real world:

"I traveled 'home' to Lake Charles, Louisiana, for a family funeral, and when my housekeeper discovered this, she shared with her team. The next evening, returning to my room after a long and especially difficult day, there was a lovely sympathy card from the hotel staff on my bed. It was such a lovely gesture, and really made my day. I just thought that sort of kindness needed to be recognized by the company." — Christi B.

"After [wondering], 'is customer service dead,'.....along comes Talisha from @springhillsuites Boston. She not only returned my youngest child's forgotten stuffed puppy, she wrote a note and took pictures of her 'extended stay.'" —@lou.romano

"During breakfast one morning I noticed one of the front desk associates helping a guest. When I went over to see what was happening I noticed papers being exchanged. This guest was from Saudi Arabia and spoke only Arabic. Since no one in our hotel could communicate with them, Keisha (the front desk employee) took it upon herself to solve the problem by going online, writing out what she wanted to say to them, translating it and then printing it out in their language for them to read. The smiles and gratitude on the guests' faces said it all." — Hotel management

"We stayed at the Courtyard recently and it was really great. The staff were very helpful and I actually had an extraordinary experience. I travel with a mobility scooter. Unfortunately, it broke down four blocks from the hotel. We were in a panic. My wife went to the hotel to find out if there was a repair place in Portland or where we could rent a wheelchair. Shortly thereafter, John Bailey from the front desk came back with a wheelchair to come to my aid. I think this was outstanding!" — @HeroesOfHospitality

"I recently found myself and my two small children stranded at Philadelphia International Airport after our flight was cancelled. We checked into SpringHill Suites in the middle of the night after a long day of travel. I immediately realized I'd run out of diapers and didn't have a car or any way to get more. Clara, the night auditor, immediately volunteered to go purchase some for me as soon as her shift ended. She went ABOVE AND BEYOND, and I am SO GRATEFUL!" —Letter to SpringHill Suites

All this demonstrates in very real, very relatable terms the power of treating others as you would want to be treated. The value in terms of motivating great customer service is obvious. What is less obvious, but even more important, is the sense of self-worth each team member gets when she or he help others. The aura it creates cannot be duplicated by other means.

Google

Remember those days before Google when you actually had to know stuff? Now if you can kind of spell it or kind of say it, Google can give you access to an answer on practically any subject you can name. That is treating others the way they want to be treated. The interesting thing is that while you as a Google user might consider yourself Google's "customer," you are not their customer in the traditional sense, that is, you don't pay Google money for using their service. Google has a whole different set of paying customers who use Google to direct their promotional and marketing messages to people who are most likely to be interested in them. And that is another innovative way to treat customers as they want to be treated.

The typical media outlet is somewhat less concerned that customers' messages reach target audiences and somewhat more concerned about delivering large audiences, many of whom might not care a bit about the marketing message being thrust at them. As a longtime media executive, I have a quick take on the value of relevance in messaging. An ad that is not relevant to the receiver is simply "clutter," while an ad that is relevant becomes "information" and often leads to additional engagement with that product or service. Sales follow. Ka-ching!

So Google has not simply built a great "search engine," it has also built a business model that increasingly funds that search engine, enabling the company to offer more and better consumer services. How could many of us find our way to new places without Google Maps, for example? And just where is Google Matchmaking to enable our children to find the proper spouses?

While there must be some concerns about the depth of knowledge Google has about each of us, the quality of the company's offerings has made the brand ubiquitous. Yes, it holds a vast quantity of personal data about virtually every Google user, some mined from our searches and some offered up by us in return for convenience. (Google has many individuals' password and credit card numbers, for example, to enable quicker transactions once a search has been completed.) Yet, Google's undergirding philosophy "Don't be evil," while not nearly as warm and inviting as "Treat others the way you'd like to be treated" or "Love thy neighbor as thyself," is certainly an acknowledgement by one of the world's biggest and most powerful companies that business success and good ethics are not diametrically opposed but are, instead, in complete alignment.

JACK R. NERAD

Marilyn the Crossing Guard

I'm thrilled to bring you the story of Marilyn the Crossing Guard, because her story proves that you don't have to be big or rich or powerful to make a positive difference on people's lives. Further, her story points out what real success is…and isn't.

Marilyn is a crossing guard who works on the corner of 17th Street and Poinsettia Avenue morning and afternoon five days a week whenever school is in session. What makes Marilyn remarkable is her relentlessly sunny nature. She is positive every time all the time, greeting each individual who crosses at her corner and waving happily to those driving by. Of course, the safety of everyone at her crosswalk is her first concern, but she makes brightening others' lives a close second. I first became acquainted with Marilyn when our children were small, and we walked them to school nearby, but now that my children are in high school and college, she has continued to be as delightful as ever as I walk my dog past her on random mornings and afternoons. And, importantly, I'm not special. She is equally kind, generous and giving to everyone who passes by.

Now I have to believe that Marilyn doesn't make a lot of money as a crossing guard. My guess is she doesn't have an immediate supervisor who insists she "give great customer service," and she doesn't get a monetary bonus for the smiles she creates. What Marilyn the Crossing Guard does is embody The GR Factor. Her compensation is not dollars-and-cents in a paycheck; it is the positive reaction she receives from everyone whose life she touches.

Again, Marilyn doesn't make a ton of money. She doesn't drive a fancy car, she doesn't live in a giant home with a prestigious address, and she doesn't take vacations to exotic locations. But what she receives as the consequence of how she lives her life is, to me, more important than that. She has her self-respect. She knows she is making a positive difference in this world. And she knows that treating others the way you want to be treated, putting The GR Factor to work, has enabled her to achieve the genuine success that so many of us spend our lives chasing. Life is not easy, and it is especially difficult for those, like Marilyn, who are born in difficult circumstances. But if you apply the GR Factor in your life, as Marilyn does, you can overcome whatever is thrown in your path.

About the Author

Jack R. Nerad has enjoyed continued success through a business career that has spanned four decades. As a business executive managing some of America's most prestigious editorial and public relations businesses, he has lived by one rule ... of treating others the way he would want to be treated. Nerad's successes stand as proof that the principle that is the foundation of The GR Factor delivers both stellar management results and a personal career path that is its own best reward.

Nerad's distinguished management career demonstrates clearly that he has uncommon expertise in getting the most from the people he works with. From global corporations to boutique firms, from startups to household names, Nerad has managed in a wide variety of organizations, each time improving the results of the business that employed him. A longtime CBS Network radio personality, Nerad has led the editorial operations of one of the nation's most iconic auto enthusiast magazines — *Motor Trend* — and one of its most iconic brands — Kelley Blue Book. He authored several well-received books, including *The Complete Idiot's Guide To Buying or Leasing a Car* and *The Complete Idiot's Guide to Hybrid and Alternate Fuel Vehicles*, as well as the true-crime book, *Fatal Photographs*. He currently serves as chief content officer of a startup publication that serves automotive shoppers, the culmination of a lengthy tenure in editorial management and public relations. Throughout his business career, helping people has been his key mission.

According to Nerad, treating people the way they want to

be treated works. It certainly worked during his 12-year tenure as Executive Editorial Director of Kelley Blue Book, where he was a key executive who helped make its website, KBB.com, the dominant auto advice resource in the United States. It worked during his 15-year career as a public relations executive for two global car manufacturers, where treating both client and the press in the manner one would want to be treated helped the companies and the brands grow. It worked during his six-year stint as Editor of *Motor Trend* magazine, where treating the reader as a close friend enabled the monthly to become the top-selling auto enthusiasts magazine.

A James Scholar graduate in Management from the University of Illinois – Chicago, Nerad has enjoyed numerous successes in radio, magazine publishing, public relations and the auto industry. As an entrepreneur he served as president/CEO/host of "America on the Road," a nationally syndicated CBS Radio show that ran for 22 years on 300 radio stations across the country. These days Nerad speaks frequently on behalf of America's car-buyers, contributing to publications that include Car and Driver, Forbes, Autobytel and Driving Today. He has often been quoted in a wide variety of prestigious publications including the *New York Times*, *Los Angeles Times*, *The Wall Street Journal* and *USA Today*. The continuing theme through his career is the ongoing attempt to follow the Golden Rule.

The critical takeaway is that, based on his record of business success, Nerad has something to say that has been time-tested. The success he has enjoyed is not a fluke; it is not the result of a random lightning strike, but instead it is the result of applying a concise and coherent set of principles that stem from both personal religious and ethical beliefs and extensive management education and experience.

The GR Factor works. It is transformative. It is powerful. It will change the way you think about others and change the way others think about you. And that change will be undeniably positive.

But for the GR Factor to deliver all it can, it must be understood that it is not a technique. It is not a policy point or a mission statement bullet. To be effective, it must be internalized; it must be embraced; and it must be lived.

Should you decide to do that, should you decide to live your life by treating others the way you want to be treated, you will discover the life-changing power the GR Factor has. And you will that find by serving others you are also serving yourself.

We wish you God's blessing in that effort.

— The Publishers, E.M. Landsea Publishers LLC, November 26, 2018

www.ingramcontent.com/pod-product-compliance
Lightning Source LLC
Chambersburg PA
CBHW031954080426

42735CB00007B/390